D1153376

REF

WITHDRAWN FROM STOCK

A Dragon Defiant

A DRAGON DEFIANT

A Short History of Vietnam

JOSEPH BUTTINGER

DAVID & CHARLES

NEWTON ABBOT

ISBN 0 7153 6064 7

Printed in Great Britain
by W J Holman Limited
for David & Charles (Holdings) Limited
South Devon House Newton Abbot Devon

Contents

Preface

The main body of this small book—four chapters on the history of Vietnam from its legendary beginnings to 1965—is based on a series of lectures I delivered in February, 1971, at the Center for Vietnamese Studies, Southern Illinois University. For an earlier treatment of the same subject, I needed three large volumes and nearly 2,000 pages to cover the same period of time. This may raise the question whether the present book really describes enough important events and deals with them fully enough to justify subtitling it even *A Short History of Vietnam*, but I am inclined to believe that a survey of the entire history of Vietnam, no matter how condensed, will be regarded, at least by some sections of the public, as a welcome addition to the hundreds of books on Vietnam that have appeared in English over the last decade.

In this vast literature, only a very few authors have dealt with history proper, and most of them have limited their coverage to more recent events, the nineteenth century being as a rule the starting

point of a story that began no later than several centuries before
the Christian era. There is almost nothing among the new literature
on nineteenth-century precolonial Vietnam, very little on the
conquest of Indochina by France, and not much more on the
colonial regime, except for the events after World War II that
led to the First Indochina War and its negotiated settlement at
the Geneva Conference in 1954. All else is concerned either with
events since 1954 or with specific aspects of Vietnamese history and
culture, such as the role of the mandarins, the life of the ethnic minorities, or the evolution of Vietnamese nationalism and Communism.
An ardent and deeply concerned reader may well have devoured
several dozen of these recent books without knowing that Vietnam
was already twice divided over a period of two centuries, or that the
Vietnamese have a tradition of fighting wars of independence that
goes back almost 2,000 years.

Although it is true that man's capacity to learn from history is
negligible, ignorance of Vietnam's past has certainly been no asset to
those who, since the end of World War II, have determined the
French and American roles in Vietnam. Even knowledge of Vietnamese history restricted to the nineteenth and twentieth centuries could have shown, to at least some of these men, how strongly
their general political approach clashed with the specific reality they
were called upon to deal with. But not only might the makers of
policy have thought twice whenever they took one of the many
decisions that finally culminated in disaster for their own countries
and for Vietnam; the public too, had it been properly informed about
a situation that was in many ways unique, might have developed
its opposition in time to stop the course that led to cruel, costly,
and senseless war.

This war is still going on, and nobody can tell when and with
what kind of settlement it will end. Crucial decisions will still have
to be made; it is to be hoped that the men called upon to make them
examine the record of French and American failures in Vietnam and
by learning at least from the recent past hasten the coming of peace

to Indochina. But this will not be the end of the debate that has so sharply divided politicians among themselves and also concerned individuals everywhere. On the contrary, this debate will again become bitter if, as seems quite possible, a united Vietnam under some kind of Communist control should in the long run emerge from the conflict.

It is this point that a better knowledge of Vietnam's entire past would again be useful, both to those who have opposed intervention in Vietnam and to those responsible for it. For I believe that a proper reading of the history of Vietnam would show to all but the very narrow-minded that the goals pursued by the French and Americans in Indochina were impossible to achieve.

Nonachievement of goals obstinately pursued is about the only common feature of the French and the American effort in Indochina. It is perfectly clear why the French fought the First Indochina War: Their aim was to regain and maintain control of a colony that they had lost in 1945. Their effort collapsed in 1954, and by losing the First Indochina War they lost, once and for all, what had been for the better part of a century their proudest colonial possession. Since reasonably conclusive judgments about their motives and aims can be pronounced, writing the history of the French post–World War II effort in Indochina presents no serious obstacles.

None of this is true for the American effort. Not only is it impossible to foresee when and how the war will end; even the obvious failure to achieve the war's goal means something different for the American effort as compared to that of the French. Unlike the French, the Americans were not defeated, which makes it questionable to describe their failure as having "lost" the war. America's effort was wasteful and certainly useless, but even those who either with satisfaction or in anger will say that it has lost the war cannot claim that the United States, like France before it, has "lost" Vietnam, not even if as a result of that failure the Communists should in the end gain control also of the South. Unlike France, the United States never owned Vietnam, and while no one can yet say with absolute certainty what the true objectives were that the different administrations in Washington pursued in Indochina, they were certainly different from the objectives of the French. All we can say is that the motives of the American leaders who made the relevant decisions in regard to Vietnam were complex and inconsistent and that the manner in which they pursued their ill-defined aims was contradictory and confused. The recently published Pentagon Papers confirm this view of U.S. policy in Vietnam.

To unravel this web of conflicting motives, senseless actions, dubious rationalizations, and conscious lies, dozens of useful books will no doubt be written, both about the decisions and actions of the immediate past and about those yet to be taken before the conflict can be said to be resolved. Not until then, and even then only after more information becomes available in memoirs of participants and new secret documents, will it be possible to describe and judge with reasonable confidence the American role in Vietnam, as I have described the role of the French in contemporary Vietnamese history in the fourth chapter of this book.

However, I do not believe that a book on Vietnam can entirely avoid dealing with the role the United States has played in the recent history of this unfortunate country. That is why I have added, to the four chapters that are a history of Vietnam up to 1965, a final chapter which, far from claiming to bring this history up to date, deals with Vietnam largely as an object of American political and military intervention. The actors in this chapter, consequently, are not only Vietnamese leaders in Saigon and Hanoi but also the men in Washington, civilian and military, elected or called upon as experts, who decided, executed, and publicly defended what they thought the United States should do in Vietnam.

Inevitably, much of the final chapter is based on the Pentagon Papers, which, although they do not contain too much that is entirely new or sensational, are so far the most comprehensive, if still incomplete, source for a description of the role the United States has played in Vietnam since World War II.

I thought it useful to precede the four chapters of historical narrative with an introductory chapter describing the country and the people, something omitted in most of the existing histories and in the many journalistic accounts of recent years that deal chiefly with political and military events. Footnotes recording and discussing my sources, as well as an annotated bibliography, should be welcome to readers whom this small book might tempt to undertake a more intensive study of a subject that has, morally and politically, preoccupied so many of us during the last decade.

A Dragon Defiant

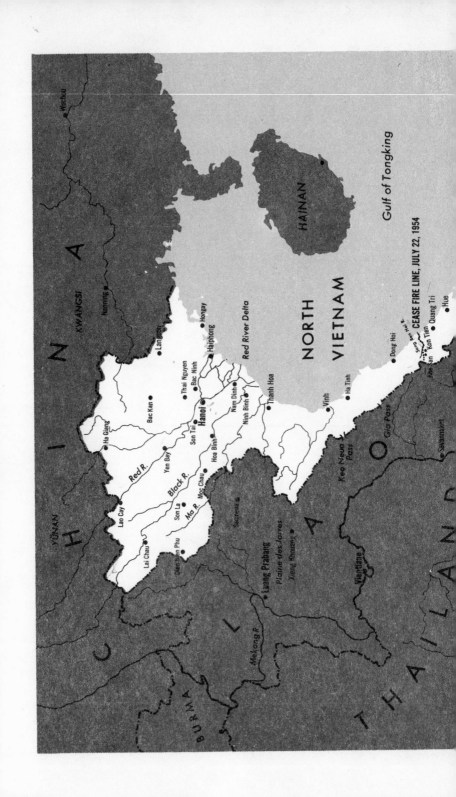

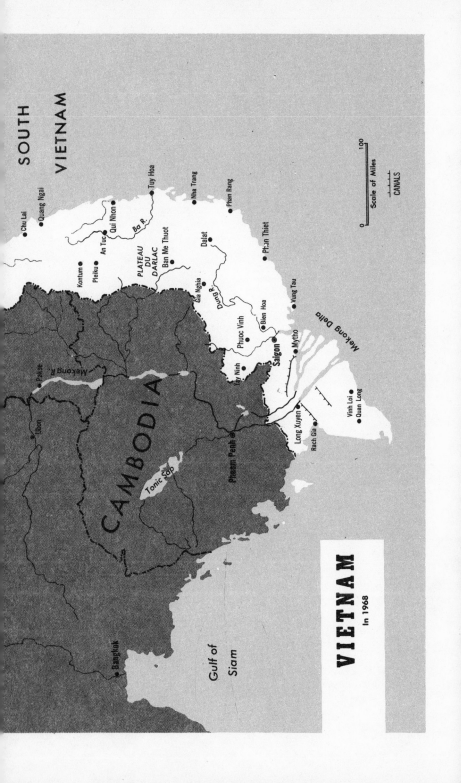

SOUTH
VIETNAM

Chu Lai
Quang Ngai

Qui Nhon
An Tuc
Ba R.
Tuy Hoa

Kontum
Pleiku
PLATEAU
DU
D'ARLAC
Ban Me Thuot
Nha Trang
Phan Rang

Dalat

Gia Nghia

Dung R.
Phan Thiet

Phuoc Vinh
Bien Hoa
Vung Tau

Saigon
Mytho
Mekong Delta

Tay Ninh

Long Xuyen
Vinh Loi
Quan Long

Rach Gia

Phnom Penh

CAMBODIA

Tonic Sap

Pakse
Mekong R.
Ubon

Bangkok

Gulf of
Siam

VIETNAM
In 1968

Scale of Miles
0   100
CANALS

I

The Land and the People

GEOGRAPHY

Anyone familiar with a description of Vietnam can hardly fail to realize to what extent the people's way of life and even the course of Vietnamese history have been determined by geographical circumstances.

Considered as a decisive influence upon the fate of a people, geography must of course be understood not as a mere description of a country's surface features, such as its mountains, plains, woodlands, rivers, and lakes, or how much of its territory is fertile and how much arid. More important are whether a country borders on one of the oceans or is landlocked, whether it lies close to or far from the equator, and whether its neighbors are small and weak or big and powerful countries. In the case of Vietnam the climate alone, wholly determined by geographical circumstances, reveals how decisively a people's life is shaped by geography. The climate determines Vietnam's vegetation and animal life, the seasonal changes of economic activity, the kind of natural catastrophes, the state of the people's health, the houses they live in, the clothes they wear, and the food they eat. And as the history of Vietnam repeatedly showed long before its contemporary tragic phase, even the periods of higher or lesser military activity are largely determined by the changing conditions the country's climate creates. Indeed, any geographical description of Vietnam will show a number of highly dramatic features, which have influenced the lives of the people and the course of history to an exceptional degree.

Uppermost among these is the fact that Vietnam, because of its geographical location, was throughout its history more exposed to the influence of China than was any other Southeast Asian country. Some of these influences were beneficial, but from a Vietnamese nationalist viewpoint, China's impact on Vietnam—military conquest, 1,000 years of foreign domination, and repeated attempts at reconquest after Vietnam had become independent in the year 939—can be described only as overwhelmingly harmful. The Indochinese peninsula, of which Vietnam occupies a narrow stretch of the eastern half, is essentially a southern extension of the Chinese land mass. A common border and contiguous coastline with China, therefore, made Vietnam much more easily accessible, by both land and sea, to its powerful northern neighbor than either Thailand in the center or Burma in the west of the peninsula.

Another important fact of Vietnam's geography is the country's unusually long coastline, which extends more than 1,400 miles along the South China Sea and the Gulf of Siam. This added significantly to the country's food supply and made the Vietnamese a nation of expert sailors. But it also exposed much of the country to devastating typhoons off the South China Sea, attracted pirates, and invited seafaring explorers and traders who frequently were only the advance guard of conquerors. During the eighth century, for instance, the Vietnamese along the coast suffered severely from three Javanese naval attacks. In the fourteenth century, the Mongols under Kublai

Khan invaded the Indochinese peninsula from the east coast; and when Western penetration of East Asia reached its climax in the nineteenth century, the attempt of the French to conquer as much as possible of the Indochinese peninsula began with naval attacks along the coast of Vietnam.

CLIMATE AND TOPOGRAPHY

For the general conditions of human existence as determined by geography, however, nothing is more important than a country's climate. The southern tip of Vietnam is only 8.3 degrees north of the equator, and the country extends more than 1,000 miles to 23.24 north latitude. If superimposed on a map of the Western Hemisphere, Vietnam's northern border would lie below Key West, Florida, and its southern border at the Panama Canal. Vietnam's climate, with the exception of high altitudes in the North, is therefore tropical all over the country. Summer temperatures differ very little between North and South. Saigon has an average summer temperature of 86 degrees Fahrenheit, compared to 85 degrees in Hanoi. But in winter, Hanoi temperatures average only 62 degrees, compared to 80 degrees in Saigon. On the mountain plateaus of South Vietnam, average temperatures are about 10 degrees lower than in Saigon. Because of its moderate climate, the city of Dalat, situated 150 miles northeast of Saigon at an altitude of 4,200 feet, became famous during the colonial period as a resort for the French and the rich Vietnamese. In the highest altitudes of the North, however, such as the Fansipan peak, which at 10,308 feet is Vietnam's highest mountain, freezing temperatures are not infrequent in December and January. But since winter coincides with the dry season, snowfall is extremely rare even on the highest peaks in the North.

One very disturbing aspect of Vietnam's climate is rainfall, important for the cultivation of wet rice, which has always constituted 90 per cent of the country's agricultural production. Rainfall is heavy but extremely irregular. The climate of Vietnam is governed by the seasonal winds of the Indian Ocean and Southeast Asia, the monsoons, which produce a dry and a wet season. During the several rainy summer months, the average rainfall in Saigon and Hanoi is 6 feet. This is almost twice the amount of the rainfall in New York in twelve months and three times the yearly rainfall in Paris. But these average amounts cannot be relied upon. Both Saigon and Hanoi have had seasons of more than 8 and of less than 3 feet of rainfall. These alternations have threatened Vietnam throughout history with either droughts or floods, both equally destructive to the rice crop and likely to reduce the people's food supply to the level of starvation.

As the floods of August, 1971, again demonstrated, this particular danger is greatest in the Red River delta of North Vietnam. This delta, which in prehistoric times was a deep gulf, was created over several millenniums by the mass of red silt that the Red River carries on its way from the Chinese province of Yünnan and the mountainous back country of North Vietnam to the Gulf of Tongking. Eight hundred miles long, the Red River, after being joined about 20 miles above Hanoi by the waters of the Clear River and the Black River, carries an average of 140,000 cubic feet of water per second toward the ocean—twice the amount of the Rhône in a bed considerably smaller. But the changes between the dry and wet seasons and the irregularity of the seasonal rainfall make this average highly theoretical. For months during the dry season, which in the North and South coincides with winter, the volume of the Red River sinks as low as 30,000 cubic feet per second. It increases during the rainy season ten-, twenty-, and sometimes fortyfold, to no less than 850,000 cubic feet per second, depending on variations in the seasonal rainfall. Contained between high dams, the waters of the Red River sometimes flow several meters above the level of Hanoi on their way through the delta. Any break in the dams is therefore bound to have catastrophic consequences for the entire delta.

What makes the Red River a permanent threat to the crops and even the lives of the people in the delta, apart from excessive rainfall, is the nature of North Vietnam's mountainous back country. Its barren heights retain little or nothing of the heavy precipitation and thus have made the Red River dangerous even in seasons of average rainfall. Steadily increasing human efforts to reduce this danger— going back to the earliest periods of Vietnamese history—have still not entirely succeeded in taming the Red River.

Vietnam's other great river is the Mekong, which created, where there once was a shallow bay, the vast Mekong delta of South Vietnam, one of the country's most fertile and most populous regions. Even today the sediments carried by the Mekong toward the South China Sea increase the coastal lands by no less than 150 feet every year.

The Mekong, which arises in the highlands of Tibet, is about 2,800 miles long. It flows from Tibet through the former Chinese province of Sikang and through Yünnan, forms the border between Thailand and Laos, passes through Cambodia, and splits into two major and several smaller branches in South Vietnam before reaching the sea.

Compared to the Red River, the Mekong could almost be called benign, largely because of the great dispersion of its waters into many branches throughout the delta and to the absorption of much of its excess waters during the rainy season by a vast lake in Cambodia, the Tonlé Sap. Nevertheless, the floods of 1961 gave evidence that the Mekong, too, can be an occasional threat to the crops and the lives of the Vietnamese peasants.

A stretch of nearly a thousand miles of coastline lies between the regions where the two great rivers of Vietnam flow into the ocean. Along this coast, numerous smaller rivers empty their erratic volumes of water into the South China Sea. Like the Red River and the Mekong, these rivers have created their own small deltas, some of which cover no more than a few square miles between the rugged mountains of Central Vietnam and the sea.

The mountains of Central Vietnam, together with those in the

North between the Red River delta and the borders of China and Laos, constitute another important geographical aspect of Vietnam. Arid mountains, jungles in lower altitudes, and only partly cultivable high plateaus make up nearly 80 per cent of the country's total surface of 127,000 square miles. The two great deltas, that of the Red River with 5,800 square miles and that of the Mekong with 8,500 square miles, cover only slightly more than 10 per cent of the surface of Vietnam. A good deal of fertile land lies south of the Red River delta in the provinces of Thanh Hoa and Vinh, and there are many small deltas along the coast of Central Vietnam down to the confines of the Mekong delta. Cultivable land also exists in the hills around the Red River delta, in some of the valleys of the mountainous North, and on the plateaus of Central and South Vietnam. But the country as a whole belies the notion, held by the early advocates of French colonial conquest in Asia, that Vietnam is exceptionally rich in natural resources.

A final feature of Vietnam's geography is the country's unusual shape—two wide deltas separated from each other by an extremely long and mostly narrow stretch of land. In the North, Vietnam reaches a width of 250 miles; in the South, the country's width varies between 100 and 120 miles. But over hundreds of miles in between, the country is no wider than 40 to 50 miles, covered largely by mountains, some of which reach directly to the sea, making passage by land between North and South extremely difficult.

The shape of the country not only explains the two distinct phases, separated by more than twenty years, of the conquest of Vietnam by the French; it also throws much light on the course of Vietnam's internal history: its periods of political division and civil war and the arduous process of creating a unified Vietnamese state. It is as if the Vietnamese people, in defiance of nature, had achieved national unity over a region seemingly destined by geography to be the territory of two separate states.

ANIMAL LIFE

Nothing unusual distinguishes Vietnam's fauna from that of many other tropical countries. Of the wild animals that inhabit the jungles, mountains, and plains of Vietnam, the best known are the tiger, the panther, the wild ox, the bear, the boar, the deer, and many kinds of monkeys and small game birds. Also to be found are a great variety of snakes, turtles, rodents, rats, some of which are as big as a house cat, and numerous insects, especially malaria-carrying mosquitoes. These last are prevalent in the mountains, one of the reasons why the ethnic Vietnamese have always refused to leave their deltas and settle in higher regions.

The country's domestic animals are the water buffalo, the goat, the pig, several kinds of fowl, the elephant, and, though extremely rare, the horse. Among the domesticated animals put to great use one should also count the silkworm.

POPULATION

The estimated population of Vietnam was 40.45 million in 1970, of whom 22.65 million live above and 18.8 million below the Seventeenth Parallel, the dividing line between the present two Vietnamese states. Although in territory considerably smaller than Thailand and only half the size of Burma, Vietnam is more populous than either. But in comparison with some other countries of similar size Vietnam does not seem to be overpopulated. Italy, whose territory is slightly smaller than Vietnam, has more than 53 million inhabitants, and Japan, not very much larger than Vietnam, has almost three times as many people (102 million in 1969).

This picture of a moderately populated country, however, changes drastically when the topography of Vietnam is taken into account. Roughly 80 per cent of the people live on only 20 per cent of the land, overcrowding the valleys and deltas as much as the most populated regions of India or Java. In the mountainous back country of the North, for instance, the population density is 32 people per square mile, in contrast to the average in the Red River delta, where it is 1,300. In some areas of the lower delta, population density reaches 3,000 per square mile. In the Red River delta as a whole, a population of more than 9 million has to live off a land area one-tenth the size of Iowa.

Similar conditions prevail in South Vietnam, where the density in the mountains is 26 per square mile, with some regions counting less than 10, compared to 1,000 per square mile in most of the coastal plains and small deltas of Central Vietnam. In the Mekong delta, the density varies between 200 and 500 per square mile but reaches 2,000 in several districts.

THE VIETNAMESE MAJORITY

As in all other Southeast Asian countries, Vietnam is inhabited by a bewildering variety of racially and culturally different people. However, 90 per cent of the country's total population is ethnic Vietnamese. The rest are ethnic minorities, consisting in the main of two categories: aborigines who inhabited the country before the ethnic Vietnamese and various racial groups that moved, over many centuries, from South China into North Vietnam.

In contrast to the minorities, the ethnic Vietnamese are both racially and culturally a remarkably unified people. As in many other countries, local dialects exist, but the Vietnamese speak only one language. In their customs, their temperament, and their outlook on life, the people of the North and the South are essentially alike. What differences do exist are no greater than can be found between northerners and southerners in several nationally united European countries.

In physical appearance too, the Vietnamese of the South differ very little from the somewhat sturdier Northerners. The average male is 5 feet 2 inches tall and weighs between 120 and 130 pounds. Dominant features are black hair, a round face, dark eyes with the Mongolian single fold of the eyelid, and a brownish skin that varies from light to medium. The women, even smaller than the men, are as a rule very slender. They usually wear their black hair long, and few weigh more than 100 pounds. Their graceful bodily movement is enhanced by their traditional flowing garment, the *ao-dai*, which consists of black or white slacks under a long-sleeved dress that is fitted to the waist, from which two panels, one in back and one in front, reach down to the heel.

The main foods of the Vietnamese are rice and fish, the latter mostly cooked into a pungent sauce called *nuoc-mam*. For the great mass of the people, such meats as pork, chicken, or buffalo meat are only rare additions to the menu. But noodle soups, vegetables, fruit, spices, and sweets made from rice gluten and coconut afford some variety in an otherwise monotonous diet. Like the Chinese, the Vietnamese eat with chopsticks.

The vast majority of the Vietnamese are still peasants. They live in villages that are subdivided into several hamlets. Their economic activity consists primarily in the seeding of rice in irrigated paddies, the transplanting of the seedlings, and the harvesting of the crop, all done by hand labor. But the Vietnamese peasants also raise fowl and pigs, plant some vegetables, and catch fish in the country's many rivers. A great many villages along the coast live entirely by fishing.

Most Vietnamese farms are small. In the Communist North (the Democratic Republic of Vietnam), agriculture is organized in farming cooperatives and some large state farms; in the South (the Republic of Vietnam) a great many farmers still have too little land or are, in spite of various land reform programs promulgated since 1956, still tenants of large landowners.

Most villagers live in small houses built of mud and bamboo with roofs of palm leaves or grass. They sleep on thin mattresses on the floor. Men and women in the country wear the same clothes—a black shirt-like garment over cotton trousers and a conical straw hat or a cloth formed into a turban as protection against sun and rain. Western-style clothes are by and large worn only in the cities.

LANGUAGE

The Vietnamese language, probably spoken in the Red River delta already before the beginning of the Christian era, is monosyllabic. Words are invariable, verbs are not conjugated, and nouns and pronouns are not declined. Different meanings of the same word are expressed by different levels of pitch. In writing the Vietnamese language, Chinese ideographs were employed in all official and most literary texts throughout most of Vietnamese history, but at present a system of writing Vietnamese in the Latin alphabet, called *quoc-ngu*, is in general use in both North and South Vietnam. *Quoc-ngu* was invented by Portuguese and French missionaries in the seventeenth century. Vocal and consonant quality as well as syllabic tone or pitch are indicated in *quoc-ngu* by diacritical marks above, below, or across a letter.

Although the Vietnamese language was greatly enriched with many Chinese literary, philosophical, administrative, and technical terms, it is basically unrelated to Chinese. The classification of Vietnamese among the linguistic groups of Southeast Asia is still a subject of controversy. The basic vocabulary of Vietnamese is Mon-Khmer, a monotonic language of the Australo-Asiatic group. But the variotonic Thai languages have modified the basic Mon-Khmer vocabulary to such an extent that some authors regard Vietnamese as a predominantly Thai language.

French, the official language up to 1954, is still spoken by the educated in both states of Vietnam, but in the South it is slowly being replaced by English as the country's second language.

RELIGION

The majority of the Vietnamese adhere to a loose form of Buddhism, but ancestor worship as prescribed by the teachings of Confucianism is still universally practiced. The Vietnamese are singularly free of religious fanaticism and capable of accommodating a variety of religious beliefs. Typical of their total absence of religious dogmatism is the Cao Dai sect of South Vietnam, whose cult consists of a mixture of Confucian, Christian, Buddhist, and Taoist creeds combined with odd practices of spiritualism. Another religious sect in the South, the Hoa Hao, has modified Buddhism for the poor peasants by eliminating anything costly from the religious ritual.

Ever since the Catholic missionaries established themselves in Vietnam at the beginning of the seventeenth century, about 10 per cent of the population has embraced the Catholic faith. The majority of the Catholics now live in South Vietnam, but according to official Hanoi figures no fewer than 1 million Catholics, or 5 per cent of the Northern population, still live in Communist North Vietnam, enjoying, if official statements can be accepted, religious freedom under the guidance of several bishops and 350 priests.

The Vietnamese celebrate a great many holidays, of which some, as for instance the birthdays of Buddha and Confucius, have religious connotations. But the most important holiday is Tet, which marks the beginning of the Lunar New Year and of spring. It usually falls in late January or early February. Holidays are almost the only occasions when these sober people indulge in the consumption of alcoholic drinks. Several holidays in honor of national heroes afford further welcome interruptions of the Vietnamese people's rather hard and dreary life.

ETHNIC MINORITIES

In contrast to the essential unity of the ethnic Vietnamese, the ethnic minorities of Vietnam display great racial differences and great differences in degree of civilization. None of the many ethnic minority groups inhabits the deltas or the small coastal plains, regions entirely occupied by the ethnic Vietnamese. Both major minority groups live in the mountainous regions of the country, the aborigines in the mountains of the southern half of Vietnam, the immigrants from China in the mountains of the North.

Because of their habitat, the ethnic minorities of the South are commonly referred to by the French term *montagnards* (mountain people). They are of mixed Australo-Negrito, Malayo-Polynesian, and Indonesian stock, and they were inhabitants of Central Vietnam before the Vietnamese penetrated these regions and pushed them permanently into the mountains. Six large groups—the Jarai, Rhade, Koho, Bahnar, Raglai, and Sedang—account for approximately half the Southern mountain people, whose total number is estimated at 800,000. The other half is split in several dozen smaller tribes, each with its own dialect. The two basic language groups are Mon-Khmer and Malayo-Polynesian. Totally cut off from the progress of Vietnamese civilization, the mountain people continue to lead a seminomadic existence and to stagnate on the cultural level of 2,000 to 3,000 years ago. Their religion still consists largely of magic and primitive superstitions.

The attitude of the ethnic Vietnamese toward the ethnic minorities has always been one of racial prejudice, openly avowed by applying the term *Moi* to all Southern mountain people. *Moi*, which in Vietnamese means savage, is now officially banned, but recent efforts to bridge the economic and cultural gap between the Vietnamese and the Southern ethnic minorities are still a long way from their professed goal.

There is evidence that progress toward the integration of the ethnic minorities into Vietnamese society has been greater in North Vietnam, whose minority population, mostly of Mongolian stock, is estimated at 2 million. These also consist of a number of major groups, such as the Thai, Tho, Man, Nung, Muong, and Meo, as well as a great many subgroups. These subgroups are especially

numerous among the Thai, who are relatives of the Thai populations of Laos and Thailand. The dialects of the ethnic minorities
in the North are all of Tibeto-Chinese origin.

Three more minority groups living in Vietnam belong neither to
the aborigines in the South nor to the mountain populations in the
North. The first is the Chinese who have settled in Vietnam, as
in all Southeast Asian countries, in the cities. They number about
1 million, most of whom now live in the South, concentrated in the
Saigon area and several other cities. The second group comprises
about 400,000 Cambodians to the southwest of the Mekong delta.
The Vietnamese authorities have long claimed that the Cambodians
are assimilated and do not recognize them as a separate ethnic group,
but this claim is hotly disputed by Cambodia. The third minority
group not belonging to either the immigrants from China or the
aborigines includes an estimated 30,000 Cham in South Vietnam.
They are the remnants of the people of Champa, a kingdom that
extended over much of Central Vietnam after the second century
A.D., but was destroyed by the Vietnamese at the end of the fifteenth
century.

AGRICULTURE, INDUSTRY, AND
URBANIZATION

In spite of great efforts at industrialization in the North and to
a lesser extent in the South, Vietnam as a whole is still essentially
an agricultural country. The vast majority of the people consequently
live in villages cultivating rice, the country's most important crop,
of which in normal times the South produces a substantial surplus.
Because of the larger population and the smaller surface of riceland, a traditional food deficit in the North has only recently been
overcome through exceptional efforts on the part of the regime.
Neither in the North nor in the South has much progress been made
in diversifying agriculture, but both halves of the country are grow-

ing some maize, potatoes, and vegetables; the South also produces sugar cane, tea, and coffee.

The South's largest export item in normal times is rubber, grown on large plantations still in French hands. There is little coal in the South and very few minerals, but different kinds of wood and hydraulic power are abundant. They are, however, still largely unexploited. All in all, the modern sector of the economy developed slowly in the South even before the war made normal development impossible. Industry, therefore, is still limited to small-scale manufacture for the local market, such as sugar, beverages, soap, pharmaceuticals, paper, cigarettes, and some textiles and building materials. Most industries in the South are situated in the Saigon area.

For two reasons, both results of the war, a great and rather unhealthy population shift from rural to urban areas has taken place in the South since 1965. First is the construction boom that set in after American intervention in the war created a need for huge military installations, especially in harbor cities such as Danang, Cam Ranh, and Saigon. This development has greatly increased the nonagricultural labor force. Second, villagers in search of security have fled from the war-torn countryside into the cities. Population figures of most cities are constantly shifting and therefore cannot be exact, not even for the capital. All that is known is that Saigon has well over 2 million inhabitants, many of them forced to live in miserable shacks, enduring abject poverty. Danang, the South's second largest city, grew from 60,000 inhabitants in 1957 to 150,000 in 1967 and was estimated to have reached half a million in 1971. Most other cities of the South have at least doubled, and some have tripled in population. Hue, the old imperial capital, which has a university but no industries, had a population of less than 30,000 after World War II. In 1967, it had 110,000. Dalat, the small resort city in the mountains northeast of Saigon, grew from less than 20,000 inhabitants in 1945 to 70,000 in 1970. The cities of Kontum and Pleiku in the highlands, of Cantho and My Tho in the Mekong delta, and especially the harbor cities Nha

Trang and Cam Ranh all have increased their population, not as a result of economic development but as an unhealthy consequence of the war.

A more natural increase of city populations took place in the North before the period of bombing between 1965 and 1968 led to mass evacuations of all major urban areas. The growth of some Northern cities since the end of the colonial period is really spectacular. Hanoi, which in 1950 still had fewer than 200,000 inhabitants, had reached 850,000 in 1965. This total, however, includes the new suburbs, which testify to the rapid industrialization the North experienced between 1955 and 1965. A similar pattern is observable in the North's second largest city, Haiphong, which grew from 70,000 in 1950 to 370,000 in 1965, also largely because of the development of industries.

Northern industry, in addition to a great variety of goods for local consumption, already produces much for export. The Hanoi regime also boasts a vast complex of steelworks at Thai Nguyen, north of Hanoi; a small but very modern shipyard at Haiphong; and the largest tool factory in Southeast Asia. The North also has large urban population centers near its several rich deposits of coal and some other minerals. Production of fertilizers, furniture, bicycles, chemicals, and canned foods, also for export, is substantial, as is that of textiles, largely concentrated at Nam Dinh in the lower Red River delta, already the site of Vietnam's biggest textile factory under the colonial regime.

Population increases due to economic progress have also taken place in other cities of North Vietnam, such as Langson, northeast of Hanoi near the Chinese border; Vietri, at the confluence of the Red, Black, and Clear rivers 20 miles northwest of Hanoi; and Lao Kai, where the Red River crosses from China into Vietnam. Much of the North's industry has been destroyed during the bombing phase of the war, but reconstruction started immediately after the halt of the bombing on November 1, 1968.

According to two generations of Vietnamese nationalists, the economic policies of the colonial regime prevented the country's economic progress by systematically obstructing industrialization. Today's nationalists in both the North and the South are convinced that, once peace is re-established, their country, whether still separated or reunited, will enter a period of rapid development of the modern sector of its economy, for which Vietnam possesses sufficient natural and human resources.

Four symbolic animals, painted, engraved, or sculptured, play an important role in Vietnamese mythology. They are the unicorn, the tortoise, the phoenix, and, of even greater importance, the dragon, a fabulous creature of Chinese-Vietnamese mythology. Dragons are immortal, and although their appearance is frightening, they do not represent evil. On the contrary, the dragon in Vietnam was always regarded as a symbol of power and nobility, and thus it became the chief attribute of the person highest in nobility and greatest in power of ancient Vietnam: the emperor or king.

2

Prehistory and Chinese Rule

ORIGINS

The first and often the most difficult questions any historian must deal with concern origins: What racial and ethnic strains contributed to the formation of a given people? How is this people related to its neighbors, and what historical forces shaped its evolution toward a distinct national identity?

Because of the prevalence of mass migrations in prehistoric and early historical times, the question of origins is often raised in a narrow geographical sense: Where did a people come from? This happened also in regard to the Vietnamese people. When some French scholars thought they had discovered where the Vietnamese people came from, they believed that they had also answered all questions concerning its origins. According to their theory, the Vietnamese are direct descendants of the so-called Viets, a people that inhabited large regions of China south of the Yangtze River.

C

Several Viet kingdoms were destroyed by the expanding Chinese empire in the year 333 B.C. The various tribes of the Viets were then gradually driven farther and farther south, and at least one of them is presumed to have entered the Red River delta, where it founded the first Vietnamese state.[1]

The fact that this theory has been abandoned does not mean that the problem it tried to deal with has otherwise been fully clarified. The number of ethnographic and archaeological studies covering the territory historically occupied by the Vietnamese keeps growing, but our knowledge about the origin of this people remains fragmentary. The Viets gave the Vietnamese their name, but they do not qualify as their sole ancestors. Ethnological and biological evidence, as well as social and cultural indications, show strong affinities between the Vietnamese and the peoples of the Indonesian and Thai racial families. It is generally assumed today that the Vietnamese as a distinct people did not enter into but were born in the Red River valley, the result of a complex racial and cultural fusion, of which the various components are not yet clearly determined.[2]

Racial diversity has always characterized the populations all over Southeast Asia, and in particular in the regions of Indochina now inhabited by the Vietnamese. Negroid pygmies are thought to have entered Indochina some 30,000 years ago. A few of their descendants are still found in Malaysia and the Philippines. They were followed by Australoid and Melanesian Negritos of the Australian and Papuan tribes. All Negritos have disappeared from Vietnam, but indications that they were the country's earliest known inhabitants have been confirmed by skulls found along the coast of the South China Sea. However, not all Negritos were pushed off the Indochina peninsula. Some must have been absorbed by later arrivals, as many racial characteristics among the mountain tribes of South Vietnam prove.

The first of the later arrivals were the Austronesians, or Indonesians, as we more commonly call them. Finds at Hoa Binh and

Bac Son belonging to the fourth and third millenniums B.C. already show a strong preponderance of Melanesian types over Negritos. This preponderance increases sharply in neolithic finds of the second millennium B.C. after the main groups of Indonesians had penetrated the Indochinese peninsula from South China.

The Austronesians were followed by two Australo-Asiatic racial families who, unlike the Austronesians, never left the mainland. The descendants of one of these groups, linguistically classified as Mon-Khmer, today inhabit Cambodia and the lowlands of Thailand and Burma. The second group, a Malayo-Polynesian people, founded, in the second century A.D., the Kingdom of Champa, located along the east coast of Indochina over an area that today comprises Central Vietnam and part of South Vietnam. It is likely that the population pressure caused by these new arrivals started the movement of the Indonesian people toward the island world of Southeast Asia. Both Australo-Asiatic linguistic groups are still represented among the mountain tribes of South Vietnam and Laos, and racial as well as linguistic characteristics show that, along with the Indonesians, these Australo-Asiatics have a share in the formation of the Vietnamese people.[3]

However, the formation of the Vietnamese as a distinct ethnic group must be put at a much later date than the second millennium B.C. Even during the Bronze Age, which in Vietnam started about 600 B.C., the inhabitants of the Red River delta were still of predominantly Indonesian stock. This is borne out by conclusive archaeological finds at Dong Son in the North Vietnamese province of Than Hoa.[4] The Dongsonians, as these proto-Vietnamese are called, brought bronze from China into the Red River delta; they are considered the last Indonesian immigrants into Indochina. Not until about three centuries later did people arrive that added the Mongolian strain to the largely Indonesian stock in the Red River delta. These were the Viets and the first waves of the numerous groups of Thai that eventually populated much of Indochina.[5]

In spite of much recent new information, our knowledge about the origin of the Vietnamese is still largely hypothetical. But that a fusion of Viet and Thai peoples with the still dominant Indonesian population of the Red River delta took place can no longer be doubted. Not only archaeological finds but language research, too, confirms the mixed racial and cultural origin of the Vietnamese. Although the Vietnamese speak a distinctly separate language, close analysis reveals it to contain important Mon-Khmer and Thai elements. Chinese, too, at a later stage in the evolution of Vietnamese civilization, enriched the Vietnamese language. The monotonic Mon-Khmer language family contributed many of the basic words to Vietnamese, the Thai languages gave it tonality and some characteristic grammatical elements, and Chinese supplied it not only with a script but also with most of its administrative, philosophical, literary, and technical terms.[6]

Further evidence for the theory that the Vietnamese people and their culture are a product of elements to be found among most peoples of Southeast Asia is provided by ethnography. In common with the people of Melano-Indonesian, Mon-Khmer, and Thai stock, the Vietnamese practiced totemism, animism, tattooing, the chewing of betel nuts, and the blackening of teeth. Marriage rituals and seasonal festivals, as well as historical legends and social organization, also confirm the very close relationship between the Vietnamese and most other peoples of Southeast Asia.[7]

The racial encounters and ethnic fusions that produced the Vietnamese people must be described as having taken place in prehistoric times. Their result was the rise of an authentic local culture in the Red River delta before its annexation by the Chinese, a culture strong enough to prevent the absorption of this people by the Chinese. But the formation of the Vietnamese people as we know it today took several more centuries. From the first century B.C. on, Chinese civilization, and to a lesser degree also Indian civilization via the states of Champa and Cambodia, were the influences that completed the process through which the Vietnamese

became a nation—a nation that no amount of historical misfortune
has been able to deprive of its proud identity.

VIETNAM BEFORE CHINESE RULE

It must be assumed that the racial and cultural fusions that
destined the proto-Vietnamese of 200 B.C. to survive as a distinct
ethnic entity had been completed when Chinese civilization, during
the first century B.C., began to exercise its powerful influence on
the inhabitants of the Red River delta.

What were the economy, the cultural life, and the social organization of this people before the Chinese, through centuries of intermarriage and the introduction of their advanced knowledge and
technology, initiated the process through which a separate Vietnamese nation became an irrevocable historical fact?

Some time soon after 200 B.C. the people of the Red River
delta advanced from the Bronze Age into the Iron Age. This does
not mean that stone implements were no longer in use: Plows and
water buffalos were still unknown, and the land was still prepared
for cultivation with polished stone hoes. But the cultivation of
wet rice was already enough advanced to make possible the extrac-
tion of two crops annually. Irrigation, still primitive, consisted
chiefly in waiting for the tides to back up the rivers for flooding the
fields. Fishing was common, and so was hunting, for which the
main weapons were spears and bows and arrows, the bronze heads
of which were dipped in poison to kill the larger animals. Elephants
were hunted for their tusks, which were traded to China for iron.

The social organization of these proto-Vietnamese was a form
of feudalism as it still existed not long ago among some of the Thai
minority populations of North Vietnam. Tribal chiefs stood at
the head of several communities, exercising absolute and hereditary
power over all civil, religious, and military institutions. They also
owned the land, keeping the masses of the peasants in virtual serf-

dom. Above this landowning aristocracy stood the king, who probably was merely the most powerful of the feudal lords.[8]

In this and in many other respects, the inhabitants of the Red
River delta differed little from most other tribes and peoples of
Southeast Asia—the Thai, the Mon-Khmer, and the Melano-
Indonesians, to whose customs, social organization, and religious
beliefs those of the Vietnamese were then still closely related.
Only several centuries after the imposition of Chinese rule did the
Vietnamese develop ethnic characteristics and civilized institutions
that separated them more and more from their neighbors and distant
relatives of the Southeast Asian world.

FROM LEGENDARY TO EARLY KNOWN
HISTORY

The extent to which Vietnamese civilization, alone among all
the countries of Southeast Asia, was shaped by Vietnam's powerful
neighbor to the north is evident in all aspects of Vietnamese life:
in the country's political institutions, the people's philosophy and
religious practices, in Vietnamese literature and art, and even in
the legends that attempt to describe the origin of the Vietnamese
people and state. Although these legends received their literary
form only during the twelfth century A.D., some 200 years after
the Vietnamese had freed themselves of Chinese political domination, they nevertheless reveal a deep awareness of the debt Vietnam
owes to Chinese civilization. According to Vietnam's most authorita-
tive legend, the history of the Vietnamese people begins with De
Minh, a descendant of a divine Chinese ruler who was also the
legendary founder of Chinese agriculture. De Minh's grandson,
Lac Long Quan, Dragon Lord of the Lac (the earliest known ethnic
designation for the Vietnamese) reconfirmed the close ties to China
by marrying a Chinese immortal, Au Co, according to legend in
order to establish peace between the Vietnamese and Chinese. Au

Co bore Lac Long Quan 100 sons before the royal couple separated. The queen moved with fifty of her sons into the mountains, while the king stayed with the remaining fifty in the lowlands, to this day the preferred habitat of the Vietnamese. Lac Long Quan's son, Hung Vuong, became the founder of the first Vietnamese dynasty, the Hong Bang, who are said to have ruled Vietnam from 2879 to 258 B.C. Legend thus makes all kings of Vietnam for 2,621 years descendants of a Chinese mother.[9]

This and several other legends reflect, in mythical terms, the fusions, conflicts, and separations of people from the North and South and from the mountains and lowlands. The immortals appear as mountain dwellers, while the inhabitants of the lowlands at the seacoast are related to dragons. De Minh's son and successor, Kinh Duang Vuong, for instance, called himself the Dragon Lord of the Sea. The retreat of Queen Au Co with fifty of her sons into the mountains has been interpreted as a mythical record of a pre-historic separation of the people in the Red River delta, possibly because of overpopulation. Those who left for the hills around the delta could have been the ancestors of the Muong who now inhabit these regions and are in fact the only ethnic minority of Vietnam related in language and customs to the Vietnamese.

In its 2,621 years of existence, the Hong Bang dynasty is said to have counted only eighteen kings, each one averaging 150 years. Even if seasons are counted as years, the story loses little of its legendary quality, which is further underlined by another claim: Vietnam, then called Van Lang, is said to have extended beyond the Red River delta and over much of South China.

The last of the Hong Bang kings is described as a loafer and drunkard. Legend has him overthrown by the ruler of Thuc, a northern neighboring state, who invaded and conquered Van Lang in 258 B.C., uniting it with Thuc and ruling it under the name Au Duong Vuong (King Au Duong) for fifty years. In the name Au Lac, which he gave the new state, the earliest designation of the Vietnamese reappears. This led to the theory that the conquering ruler of Thuc was not the head of a foreign state but the chief of a northern province of Van Lang.[10]

There is some evidence that a Vietnamese kingdom called Au Lac existed, although its boundaries are unknown.[11] Ironically, the near certainty of its existence rests on the knowledge we have of its demise, which occurred in the year 208 B.C. This event is recorded in Chinese annals and can be regarded as the first verified date of Vietnamese history, marking the end of the period for which we must rely on legend for a glimpse of prehistoric Vietnam. In 208 B.C., the Red River delta and the country south of it down to present-day Danang, which may have been the territory of Au Lac, became part of the kingdom of Nam Viet.

Nam Viet came into existence when a Chinese general, Trieu Da, exploited the crisis that led to the fall of the Chinese dynasty of the Ch'in by making himself the ruler of a state covering much of South China. The capital of Nam Viet was in the vicinity of present-day Canton. Trieu Da had all officials loyal to the Chinese emperor executed. He adopted the customs of the Viets, who after the destruction of their old kingdom in 333 B.C. inhabited much of South China, and he and his successors ruled over their large non-Chinese state almost 100 years. The Vietnamese lands were the southernmost provinces of his dominion. Trieu Da ruled these regions indirectly, leaving the local chieftains in control of the population under the supervision of a royal delegate in each of the two provinces into which Au Lac was divided.[12]

Soon after the founding of Nam Viet, in the year 202 B.C., China was reorganized under the Han dynasty, with which Trieu Da and his successors waged ninety years of diplomatic and military battles. Nam Viet was conquered by the great Han emperor Wu-ti in 111 B.C. It was divided into nine military districts headed by Chinese officials. Three of the districts comprised the territory of former Au Lac, approximately what today is North Vietnam. This was the beginning of more than 1,000 years of Chinese rule, during which Vietnam was commonly referred to by its new masters as the province of Giao Chi.

FUNAN AND CHAMPA

Neither as Nam Viet nor under Chinese rule did the territories occupied by the Vietnamese extend below the vicinity of present-day Danang. What happened during those centuries in the lands farther south, which today we know to be no less Vietnamese than the country's northern half?

While in the North the formation of the Vietnamese people was completed under the influence of Chinese civilization, the territories of present-day South Vietnam, populated by descendants of the Australo-Asiatic migrants into Indochina, saw the birth of two states distinctly different from the one that a few centuries earlier had arisen in the Red River delta. These two states were Funan and Champa, both of which resulted from Indian penetration into Indochina.

Funan, which was founded during the first century A.D., covered the entire Mekong delta and most of present-day Cambodia. It was a powerful state with a strong fleet. A Chinese diplomatic mission around A.D. 250 reported that Funan had an administration almost as adroit in collecting taxes as the Chinese themselves. The Chinese also found many walled cities and great palaces in Funan, and they were surprised to discover that the people, most of whom they described as "black, ugly, and almost naked," had books and archives, which the Chinese thought they alone possessed.

But unlike the new civilization that developed in the Red River valley as a result of Chinese military conquest, the Indianized state and civilization of Funan were not created by any kind of military action, Indian or otherwise. It was entirely the product of Indian cultural and economic penetration. Lively commercial relations between India and the southern half of Indochina existed long before the rise of Funan, whose upper class created a state and culture on principles developed in India and carried to Indochina by Indian merchants, priests, and literati. Indian art and philosophy flourished in Funan, and its religious life was characterized by the adoption of Sanskrit as the country's sacred language.[13]

Most of these cultural features were found also in Champa, which, according to Chinese annals, was founded in A.D. 192. Champa covered the east coast of Indochina from the confines of the Mekong delta as far north as the mountain ridge of Hoanh Son, near the so-called Gate of Annam at the Eighteenth Parallel. It included in the north a whole province of formerly Chinese-occupied Giao Chi (Vietnam), lost to aggressive Champa during a period of Chinese imperial decline, when the Cham waged border wars in the north and even attacked the coast of China.

Champa too had a powerful fleet, important for its economy because the Cham lacked sufficient cultivable land for the development of agriculture. But their fleet served not only commerce; it was used also in plundering campaigns against Champa's neighbors. And because the Cham conducted, from hidden bays, attacks on trading ships all along the Indochina coast, they have been called not only a warlike but even a semipiratical people. Nevertheless, Champa had a highly developed civilization. The extent to which its art and architecture were the result of Indian influences can be seen in the collection of Cham art in the museums of Danang and in the architectural ruins of a Cham city in the province of Quam Nam.[14]

Funan, which had dominated much of Indochina for several centuries, disappeared during the sixth century A.D. It was absorbed by a people descending from farther north, the Mon-Khmer, or Cambodians, who in the next few centuries created the most powerful empire known to have existed on the Indochinese peninsula.

Although the people of Funan occupied a region that in the course of history became a vital part of Vietnam, they probably had no direct contact with the Vietnamese, who penetrated the former heartlands of Funan only about 900 years after the conquest of Funan by the Mon-Khmer. Whatever influence the Indianized culture of Funan had on Vietnam was exercised via Champa and, later, Cambodia.

Champa lasted almost 1,000 years longer than Funan. It was

a strong and usually hostile neighbor of Vietnam when the Vietnamese made themselves independent of China in the tenth century
A.D. Champa's aggressiveness and Vietnam's need for territorial
expansion led to constant armed conflicts between the two countries,
which, after some 500 years, ended with the destruction of Champa.

VIETNAM AS A CHINESE PROVINCE

After the conquest of Champa was completed in the sixteenth
century, Vietnam was no doubt the most powerful state of Indochina. But as a unified and assertive nation, the Vietnamese, who
in their historical "March to the South" later also conquered much
of Cambodia, can hardly be said to have existed when the Chinese
became their masters in 111 B.C. The Vietnamese became the distinct and self-assured nation that finally occupied the entire east
coast of Indochina only several centuries later—centuries of complex
interaction between Chinese rule and Vietnamese responses to it.
The evolution toward final Vietnamese national identity, a very
involved process full of contradiction, can best be described in an
apparent paradox: The more the Chinese labored to deprive this
people of its ethnic identity, the faster they promoted the development of a Vietnamese national consciousness until, halfway through
the thousand years of Chinese rule, the point was reached from
which this people, as I have said elsewhere, could no longer become
"anything other than its own riper self."[15] Indeed, it is the story
of Vietnam under Chinese domination that contains the explanation
of the ethnic durability and the irrepressible national vitality of
the Vietnamese.

Before describing how this surprising result came about, it must
be pointed out that even from a narrow Vietnamese nationalist
viewpoint, Chinese rule cannot be regarded as a purely negative
experience for Vietnam. During the many centuries of Chinese
political domination and economic exploitation, the Vietnamese

also benefited from the advanced and then still progressing civilization of China. It was through the adoption of the technical skills,
the administrative achievements, and the high degree of learning
of the Chinese that the Vietnamese, at the end of Chinese rule,
had become, next to Cambodia, the most advanced nation of the
Indochinese peninsula.

The innovations that the Chinese brought into the Red River
valley soon after their conquest of Nam Viet were many. They
improved local agriculture through better methods of irrigation,
building dams and canals, and caring for their supervision and up-
keep. They introduced the plow and water buffalo and brought
many new tools and weapons. The art of pottery was advanced,
and new techniques of mining were applied. To be sure, the roads,
waterways, and harbors the Chinese constructed were planned to
facilitate communications with the newly acquired lands and to
insure their administrative control. But control, to begin with, was
loose. There was little interference with local customs or even with
the local administration. The old hereditary lords continued to
exercise their traditional control of the peasant population, just
as they had when their country was still a province of Nam Viet.
The military districts into which Giao Chi was divided were headed
by Chinese governors, whose posture of noninterference with local
customs and local administration made Vietnam a leniently governed
Chinese protectorate.

This policy, however, was bound to come into conflict with the
logical course of Chinese imperial rule, which had a long tradition
of not only economic development of newly conquered territories
but also successful assimilation of the populations taken into the
empire. Sooner or later political power would be employed to achieve
Sinicization through the systematic imposition of Chinese customs
and learning, and through intermarriage with the local population.

In Giao Chi, this inevitable course was initiated at the beginning
of the Christian era under an energetic central governor who realized that the local chiefs and their continued control over the

population prevented both economic development and cultural assimilation of the province. It is safe to assume that there was a strong tendency on the part of the Chinese empire to exploit the fertile Red River delta and its mountainous hinterland, thought to be rich in rare minerals, great forests, and sources of ivory. But no less valuable was the new province as a stopover for China's maritime trade, which the Han dynasty had begun to conduct with the Spice Islands of Southeast Asia, India, and even the Near East. Chinese vessels and others from many distant countries docked at the harbors along the northern Indochinese coast. The ever widening contacts with the outer world and the new goods and new ideas that came into the Red River delta promoted a steady modernization of the country. Economic, administrative, and cultural functions developed, which the local lords were unfit to discharge. More and more Chinese officials were brought into Giao Chi with the aim of establishing direct and firm Chinese rule.

The policy of ruling the province directly would have hurt only the old local ruling class, had it not been for the simultaneous efforts to transform the people into Chinese, efforts that had been successful elsewhere over several hundred years of Chinese imperial expansion. Vietnamese institutions were replaced by Chinese, and Chinese customs and rites were imposed by force. Even Chinese clothing and hairdress were made obligatory, much to the annoyance of the local population. Together with their language, which replaced the local speech in all official dealings, the Chinese also spread Taoist religious concepts and strict Confucian learning.

Developments in China early in the first century A.D. favored the policy of Sinicization in the Red River delta. The Han dynasty, which ruled China from 202 B.C. to A.D. 220, was temporarily eclipsed by a usurper from A.D. 9 to 23. This event created a mass of political refugees—officials, scholars, officers, and soldiers who fled China to escape persecution by the new regime. They fled southward into the distant province of Giao Chi, whose governor had refused to recognize the new central authority. Thousands

of highly qualified men thus became available to the governor of
Giao Chi. They enabled him to replace more and more of the local
lords with Chinese officials and to intensify his policy of spreading
Chinese ideas and Chinese ways of life.

After only a few decades of direct rule and forced Sinicization,
discontent led to the first local uprising against the Chinese. This
was the much celebrated rebellion of the Trung sisters, which broke
out in A.D. 39. Trung Trac was a noblewoman whose husband
had been executed by the Chinese. She and her sister Trung Nhi
led the tribal chiefs and their armed followers in attacks on the
Chinese garrisons, and after overwhelming them proclaimed themselves queens of an independent Vietnamese state. Their kingdom
lasted only three years. A strong army sent by the Han emperor
re-established Chinese rule in A.D. 42.

This Vietnamese defeat marked the end of all traces of local
autonomy. Many of the local chieftains were killed, and hundreds
of others were deported to China, while those remaining, in order
to survive, submitted to the Chinese, adopted Chinese customs,
and eventually were even permitted to serve in the Chinese-
dominated administration.

It has been argued that the uprising of the Trung sisters failed
because it was a movement restricted to the local aristocracy, un-
supported by the masses of the peasants. While it is no doubt
significant that the movement originated among the old upper
class, it is unlikely that it could have achieved even its temporary
success without popular support. Its defeat must be ascribed not to
local political causes but to the overwhelming military power of
the Chinese empire. It will be seen that lasting Vietnamese independence was finally achieved at a time when China lacked the
military means to subdue the rebellious province at the empire's
southern periphery.

What a weakening of Chinese military power might one day
mean for the political fate of the people in the Red River delta
became apparent long before the actual achievement of Vietnamese

independence in the tenth century. At the end of the second century A.D., when the Han dynasty, prior to its fall in A.D. 220, went through several decades of decline, the Chinese governor Che Sie, who headed the province of Giao Chi from A.D. 187 to 226, made himself virtually independent of China. After the fall of the Han, the Chinese empire was split into three contending kingdoms. Che Sie maintained formal relations with the heads of the Wu, who ruled South China from Nanking, but he governed the province in the manner of an independent king. When he died, his son proclaimed himself his successor and, on hearing that the court at Nanking would not confirm him, began to make military preparations to defend the autonomy of Giao Chi, which his father had established.

Although the self-appointed governor was quickly defeated by an army of the Wu, his attempt to make Giao Chi a semi-independent region of the empire marks an important stage in the historical process that led to the re-establishment of a separate and genuine Vietnamese state. Che Sie had considered himself no longer subject to imperial orders, but he and his followers at the head of Giao Chi continued the policy of systematic Sinicization. During Che Sie's time, but also later, this policy was again greatly aided by the influx of thousands of refugees, many from the class of scholar-officials (mandarins), who fled China during the civil disorders that preceded and followed the fall of the Han dynasty. Up to the year 590, six warring dynasties fought for control of the Chinese empire. In spite of the policy of Sinicization, and partly even as a result of it, social and political developments took place during these centuries in Giao Chi that strengthened the tendencies toward local autonomy. First of all, the masses of the peasants, probably 90 per cent of the population, were little affected by the measures applied to transform the Vietnamese into Chinese. They did not reject Chinese technical innovations but resisted the imposition of Chinese customs. One reason for their resistance to Sinicization was no doubt the strength of the local culture, as it had developed in their long pre-Chinese ethnic past. Another reason must have been the sameness of their entire economic and social existence as rice-producing peasants. The peasants worked now, just as they had before the coming of the Chinese, for large land-owners, under virtually unchanged conditions of life.

This was not true for the old local ruling class, which underwent profound changes as a result of Chinese political rule. But these changes too, in ways certainly unforeseen by the promoters of Sinicization, strengthened the tendencies toward local autonomy and eventual independence. After the defeat of the Trung sisters, more and more Chinese officials on all levels of the administration were given large landholdings taken from the rebellious members of the former aristocracy, landholdings that the Chinese officials soon succeeded in making hereditary. Together with the members of the local upper class who cooperated with the Chinese and accepted Chinese customs and learning, these officials formed a new local elite, whose interests were not always identical with those of a distant imperial court. Their wish to live well by the labor of the peasants clashed with imperial demands for high tributes from the conquered province. Furthermore, these Chinese officials, most of whom had arrived as single men, had married into the local aristocracy, which in time must have diluted their purely Chinese outlook and established a community of interests with the Sinicized upper strata of Vietnamese society. In fact, while the Vietnamese upper class submitted to some extent to the ways of the Chinese overlords, the Chinese officials underwent what one is tempted to call a process of Vietnamization. A Sino-Vietnamese upper class developed, of which the Chinese governor Che Sie might be regarded as a forerunner.

The most representative exponent of this class was an official by the name of Ly Bon, who, although himself of Chinese ancestry, staged a great anti-Chinese rebellion about 400 years before full independence was achieved. Ly Bon established a genuine Vietnamese kingdom after driving the Chinese out of Giao Chi in 542.

Like the Trung sisters 500 years before him, he was defeated by Chinese armies after only three years in power, but some of his followers held out in the northern mountain regions until A.D. 603.

Between the sixth and tenth centuries, the Vietnamese people, under the leadership of its Sino-Vietnamese upper class, staged several more rebellions,[16] but Chinese power precluded lasting success as long as China was competently ruled, between 618 and 907, by the great T'ang dynasty. Only after the fall of the T'ang did the prospects of liberating Vietnam from Chinese rule suddenly improve. A series of uprisings early in the tenth century culminated in a decisive defeat of a Chinese army in 939, the year from which the Vietnamese commonly date the beginning of their national independence.[17]

D

3

Independence and Expansion

THE TROUBLED BEGINNINGS OF INDEPENDENCE

It is not at all surprising to learn that, in 939, after wars of liberation that had raged, on and off, for three decades, Vietnam was an exhausted country, devastated over wide regions and deprived of many of its best young men. Still, the achievement of independence, after more than 1,000 years of Chinese rule, must have caused great and universal joy, even if the material benefits and the higher social status promised by independence remained restricted to a small minority. Peasants in remote villages may not have been greatly affected by the changes in the fortunes of their country, but the end of a long period of wars on their soil was for the whole people an immediate and welcome relief. Also, the satisfaction derived from the triumph of their national aspirations was most likely shared even by the humblest of the nation. To be rid of a foreign government whose commands and requests had been a hardship for countless generations could not but raise hopes for a better life.

But for the great majority of the Vietnamese people, these hopes, never fully realized, were most cruelly disappointed during the first half-century after the departure of the Chinese. The reason was not so much the continuing danger of reannexation by China, which was revived when the Sung dynasty, in 960, began to re-organize the shattered Chinese empire. The Vietnamese people suffered, and independent Vietnam was unable to prosper, because it lacked for several decades the blessings of internal peace.

The first ruler of newly independent Vietnam was Ngo Quyen, the general who had defeated the Chinese in 939.[18] He became the founder of the first authentic Vietnamese dynasty, the Ngo dynasty. In order to emphasize the continuity of a Vietnamese national existence, he set up his capital at the site from which the country had been ruled before it became a province of China.[19] Ngo Quyen was a competent ruler, but he died in 944 without having completed the task of setting up a strong central administra-tion, badly needed to hold down the feudal lords whose greed and lust for power threatened to split the country into numerous private domains. Ngo Quyen's heirs are reported to have been feeble men. By 966, Vietnam was in a state of anarchy. A dozen autonomous local chiefs fought one another for more territory to control and exploit; and an effective central authority capable of looking after the needs of the people and the state no longer existed.

The Ngo dynasty, fortunately, was overthrown in 968, allegedly by a man of peasant stock, Dinh Bo Linh, who became the founder of the Dinh dynasty. Bo Linh was a powerful personality and proved to be a capable ruler. Within a few years, he had defeated the con-tentious feudal lords in a series of civil wars and reunited the country under the name Dai Co Viet. Local chiefs who defied his authority faced the prospect of being boiled in oil or fed to the king's tigers. Instead of ruling with the help of the old aristocracy, Bo Linh set up a hierarchy of civil and military officials directly responsible to him. He averted the danger of a Chinese invasion by paying high tribute to the Sung emperor. But Bo Linh, too, had a short life. After several members of his family had been assassinated by the many enemies he had made, the Dinh dynasty, in 980, was reduced to a six-year-old king, just when the Sung in China decided to complete the reorganization of the empire by sending an army into the Red River delta.

In the face of this danger, the head of the army, Le Hoan, deposed the six-year-old king and made himself ruler of Vietnam. Le Hoan, the founder of the so-called Earlier Le dynasty, defeated the Chinese in 981 and even obtained, in exchange for tribute, formal recognition for Vietnamese independence from the Sung emperor. Le Hoan was equally successful in averting an invasion of his country by Champa. He ruled from 980 to 1005, but under his successors the Earlier Le dynasty was overthrown only four years later. In the first seventy years of independence, Vietnam had thus used up the energies of three dynasties, every one of them founded by an extraordinary man but succeeded by men lacking the ability to rule their troubled country.

FOUR CENTURIES OF STABILITY AND PROGRESS

A lasting change for the better came about under the next dynasty, the Ly. The first of the Ly kings ruled eighteen years, the second twenty-six, the third again eighteen, and the fourth, Ly Nhan Ton, a full fifty-five years. All together, the Ly dynasty headed the state 215 years, from 1009 to 1224.

At least during the first half of its reign, the Ly dynasty was immensely successful in consolidating the monarchy by creating again a strong central administration capable of subduing the disruptive ambitions of the feudal lords. The divisive lords were systematically replaced at all levels of the administration by state officials trained in a civil service institute set up in 1076. After the Chinese model, the Ly, in 1089, established a fixed hierarchy of officials with nine degrees of civil and military mandarins. Political stability at last provided conditions of economic progress for Dai Viet, the new name the Ly gave to the country. The construction of a road network connecting the main cities was begun as early as 1044, and a postal service for the whole country was established soon afterward. The Ly built many dikes and canals and were altogether famous as promoters of agriculture. They moved the capital back to Hanoi, then called Thang Long.[20] They also promoted Buddhist learning, already introduced into Vietnam long before independence.[21] In spite of their firm opposition to Chinese political interference, the art and literature favored by the Ly were essentially Chinese in character.

The progress Vietnam made under the Ly, however, could have been considerably greater had not stability and prosperity been constantly threatened by the necessity of conducting foreign wars. Like Le Hoan before them, they had to fight off a new Chinese attempt to reconquer Vietnam. In 1057, a Chinese army moved toward the Red River delta. It was met by the Vietnamese on Chinese soil and defeated in a war that lasted four years. While the Vietnamese struggled in the North against the danger of falling again under Chinese rule, Champa invaded their country's southern provinces. Cambodia, which at that time had become the strongest power in Indochina, supported Champa against Vietnam. The southern provinces of Dai Viet were lost and regained several times in wars with Champa, usually lasting several years. Cambodia and Champa attacked again in 1128, 1132, and 1138 and invaded Vietnam five more times between 1138 and 1216.

Long before the end of the last of these wars, it had become evident that the Ly dynasty was no longer able to produce competent and respected rulers. The last of the Ly was a psychopath who was forced to abdicate in favor of his seven-year-old daughter.

The decline of the Ly led to a long period of civil wars, which ended in 1224 with the victory of Tran Thai Thong, head of the family who founded the second great Vietnamese dynasty, the Tran.

The Tran, whose rule lasted from 1225 to 1400, remained true to the pattern that showed the early rulers of every dynasty vigorous and gifted, only to be followed, sooner or later, by kings deplored as "sapless and feeble." However, the Tran, for more than 100 years, successfully pursued the political and economic course that had made Vietnam strong under the better rulers of the Ly. This was especially true in regard to the Tran's agrarian policy, which aimed at protecting existing riceland and adding new land through the clearing of jungles and the draining of swamps. Tran Thai Thong, the first of the Tran rulers, had the dikes of the Red River extended all the way to the ocean. Like the Ly before them, the Tran had to defend Vietnam against repeated attacks by Champa, but they succeeded several times in arranging for long periods of peaceful coexistence with some Cham rulers.

However, the greatest threat to the rule of the Tran and to the existence of the state of Vietnam continued to come from the north. After the Mongolian armies of Kublai Khan had invaded and taken much of China in the middle of the thirteenth century, their leader decided to outflank the Chinese, who held out in South China under the Sung, by invading the Red River delta. In 1257, a Mongolian army sacked Hanoi, but heat and disease, as well as heavy attacks by the Vietnamese, forced the invaders to leave Vietnam.

The failure of this invasion unfortunately did not mean that Vietnam would thereafter be safe from further Mongolian attacks. After Kublai Khan had conquered all of China and replaced the Sung in 1279, he launched an imperialist enterprise greater than any undertaken either before or after him. He wanted to connect his Far Eastern possessions by sea via India, Persia, and the Middle East with the western outposts of his empire. To make this route safe, Kublai Khan needed strategic positions in the Indonesian archipelago, which required a measure of control, if not conquest, of the Muslim kingdoms that had spread via India into Southeast Asia. To achieve this aim, the Mongolian masters of China first invaded Champa and Cambodia, only to learn that these positions were difficult to hold without control of the Red River delta. When the Tran rulers refused to let his armies pass through their territory, Kublai Khan decided to subdue the Vietnamese and annex their country. A Mongolian army, said to have numbered 500,000 men, invaded the Red River delta in 1284, no doubt confident that this small country would be unable to resist a military power that had conquered the Chinese empire. Yet the invaders succumbed to the armies of the Vietnamese, effectively supported by the ubiquitous malaria-spreading local mosquitoes. Vietnamese resistance also defeated another Mongolian invasion three years later. The general who led the Vietnamese armies during these dreadful years, Tran Hung Dao, is to this day venerated in both North and South Vietnam as one of the greatest heroes of Vietnamese history.

Before Vietnam could recover from the devastation caused by the Mongolian armies, the perennial conflict with Champa was resumed. Champa suffered a series of defeats during the last decade of the thirteenth century and was even made, after 1312, a feudatory state of Vietnam. But under the reign of King Che Bong Nga Champa freed itself in 1326 and was soon strong enough to again invade Vietnam. In 1371, a Cham army actually reached and pillaged Hanoi.

As a result of these endless wars, which exhausted the country's resources, Vietnam experienced a deep economic and social crisis. Toward the end of the fourteenth century, widespread famine fostered innumerable local revolts. The Tran dynasty, whose last ruler was also a child, was no longer able to govern effectively. It was overthrown by the regent of the young king, Ho Qui Ly, who usurped the throne in the year 1400.

TEMPORARY LOSS OF INDEPENDENCE

In 1407, seven years after Ho Qui Ly's assumption of power, the Chinese, under the great Ming dynasty, which had ousted the Mongols in 1368, reconquered Vietnam.

Why did the Ming succeed where the Sung and the Mongol rulers of China had failed? Ho Qui Ly was a first-rate general, and he is said to have mobilized a greater army against the Chinese than Vietnam ever had, either before or after him. He failed because Vietnam, after 1400, was deeply divided. A substantial part of the people were unwilling to rally to their country's defense, and many even sided with the enemy.

Ironically, this fateful condition for Vietnam was largely the result of the measures Ho Qui Ly took to save the country. After decades of war with Champa and of Tran misrule, Vietnam was financially insolvent and economically in disarray. Ho Qui Ly was a bold reformer, and he knew what had ruined the country's economy and finances. The root of all troubles was the policy of the Ly and Tran of rewarding their high officials with land, usually for life. But these landholdings not only gradually became hereditary, they also grew ever larger at the expense of the defenseless peasantry. Before 1400, the peasants constituted a class of poverty-stricken serfs and a mass of landless people who roamed the country as vagabonds, starving, stealing, and when leadership was available fighting in local rebellions. The reverse side of this picture was the existence of a class of rich and arrogant feudal landlords, interested in exploiting the peasants for their own benefit, with no regard for the needs of the state.

Like all great leaders of Vietnam, Ho Qui Ly understood that a sound agrarian policy was the key to the country's economic well-being and political stability. Only a prosperous and taxable peasantry could supply the resources needed to revive the power of the state and reduce the causes of social unrest. To this end, Ho Qui Ly decreed a radical limitation of all landholdings, distributing the lands thus obtained to the landless peasants, who then paid rent to the state. His aim was not only to make the state solvent once again but also to curb the selfish and politically disruptive ambitions of the feudal landlords.[22]

Although Ho Qui Ly's agrarian policy in the long run would have restored both the country's economic health and the power of the state, its immediate political effects were disastrous. Most of the landlords whose holdings had been radically reduced rallied behind the deposed Tran family, who, in a desperate attempt to regain royal power, appealed to the Ming for Chinese help. The Ming emperor complied, promising to put a Tran back on the throne. The treacherous help of the Tran and their followers, and the over-taxed peasantry's lack of enthusiasm for Ho Qui Ly, enabled the Ming to defeat him. Instead of re-establishing Tran rule, the Ming set up a direct Chinese administration. When the Tran called on the people to rise against the Chinese, Vietnamese resistance was drowned in blood.

The rule of the Ming was worse than anything the Vietnamese had experienced during previous attempts to make them Chinese. Besides ruthlessly exploiting the country, the Ming rulers took radical measures to denationalize the Vietnamese. Schools were permitted to teach only in Chinese. All local cults were suppressed. What national literature Vietnam had produced was confiscated and shipped to China. The women were forced to wear Chinese dress, the men to wear long hair; in order to tighten control of the people, an identity card was issued to every citizen. After ten years of Ming rule, it was clear to every Vietnamese patriot that the survival of their people, more than ever before, depended on their ability to free themselves from Chinese domination.

It is the evidence of history that, at the beginning of the fifteenth century, the evolution of the Vietnamese nation was sufficiently advanced to doom all efforts to make it Chinese. Ming rule only strengthened the nationalist sentiments of the Vietnamese and made them determined to regain national independence at any cost.

A movement to throw off the Chinese yoke started in 1418, in the province of Thanh Hoa south of the delta. It was led by a rich landowner, Le Loi, whose family, according to Vietnamese annals, numbered more than 1,000. It took ten years of bitter struggle to make Vietnam free again. The Chinese, defeated all over the country, held on to the fortress of Hanoi for almost a year, but when Le Loi defeated two armies sent to relieve them, they surrendered and were permitted to leave the country early in 1428. Le Loi pushed aside the claims of the Tran family and, under the name of Le Thai To, became the founder of the next great dynasty, the Later Le, which although only nominally in power after 1600 was to last until 1787.

EXPANSION AND DIVISION OF VIETNAM

Like the Ly and Tran 400 and 200 years earlier, the new Le dynasty under Le Thai To and his immediate successors introduced many needed reforms. One was a general redistribution of land among the entire population. Only the lands of great landowners who had collaborated with the Chinese were expropriated. The redistribution was unequal, since deserving officials and generals were rewarded with acreage enabling them to live according to their elevated status. This left not enough land for the land-hungry peasants. Lack of land, therefore, was one powerful incentive behind some internal measures of the Le, as well as behind their foreign policy. All idle fields and all lands left fallow by the great landowners were confiscated by the state and given to anyone willing to put them to use. The army was employed in deforestation to gain new riceland, much of it retained as communal to be distributed yearly among the peasants of the village. To protect the existing land, a permanent staff of dike inspectors was created. When the growth of new large landholdings threatened again to turn the smaller owners into serfs, Le Thanh Tong, who ruled from 1459 to 1497, made sure that the annually repartitioned communal lands became inalienable and untransferable.

However, population increase made all these measures insufficient. In order to gain new land, the Le rulers of the fifteenth
century inaugurated the policy of systematic territorial expansion,
a policy through which Vietnam reached its present size in 1757. In
their first great push of the "March to the South," the aim of the
Vietnamese rulers was to wrest from Champa the many small but
fertile deltas along the coast south of the Eighteenth Parallel. An
unending series of wars ensued, as a result of which Champa was
almost entirely wiped out by 1471. Vietnamese soldier-peasant
villages were created on the newly conquered territories, and masses
of landless peasants settled during the following decades all the
way south to the vicinity of present-day Nha Trang. After Champa
was eliminated, the Vietnamese began to penetrate the thinly populated Mekong delta, which the Cambodian empire, in decline since
the thirteenth century, was no longer able to defend.[23] The Vietnamese reached Saigon shortly before 1700 and annexed the rest of
the South during the following sixty years.

Among the other achievements of the great Le rulers of the
fifteenth century was the elaboration of a legal code more advanced
than any other in Southeast Asia. It gave women equality with
men in almost all respects. Education, too, was radically reformed,
making it possible for talented children of the poor to attend state
colleges along with the sons of the rich landowners and mandarins.
Le Thanh Tong founded many hospitals where patients were treated
free. Idle monks were put to work, and the building of new temples
was forbidden by some of the more economy-minded rulers. The
first of the Le monarchs were indeed ahead of many ruling princes
in Europe, as intellectuals no less than as administrators. Paper
money, for instance, had already been introduced by Ho Qui Ly
250 years before it became known in Europe.

In view of these achievements, it must come as a surprise to learn
that, after the first century of Le rule, the history of Vietnam over
the next 150 years can be described only as one period of permanent
crisis. The last able Le ruler was Hieu Tong, who died young in

1502. During the next twenty-five years, the country had no fewer
than eight different kings (or emperors, as some call them), six of
whom were assassinated by royal relatives or ambitious lords in
fights for control of the rudderless state. One of these lords, Mac
Dang Dung, former governor of Hanoi, came out on top after years
of bloody struggles. He walked on a staircase of lordly and royal
corpses right up to the throne, which he reached in 1527. Another
ambitious lord, Nguyen Kim, made himself the champion of the
deposed Le dynasty. He set up a rival government-in-exile in Laos
during 1532 and started a civil war against Mac Dang Dung. By
1545, Nguyen Kim had won the southern half of the country up to
Thanh Hoa. He was murdered, and his place was taken by the head
of the lordly family of the Trinh, who waged almost sixty years of
war before Mac Dang Dung was driven out of Hanoi in 1592.

Of much longer duration than this first division of Vietnam was
a second one, which came about around 1620, largely the result
of Vietnam's extension southward, which made it increasingly
difficult to rule the country effectively from Hanoi. The expanding
provinces in the south had been governed from Hue, in the name of
the Le, by the lordly family of the Nguyen even since 1560. In
Hanoi, all power was in the hands of the Trinh, who, after the
ouster of Mac Dang Dung, had made themselves "hereditary princes
in charge of government," depriving the monarch of any real power.
The Nguyen, no less power-hungry than the Trinh, refused obedience to Hanoi after 1620, pointing out that they owed obedience
not to the ruling Trinh but to the virtually deposed Le. The Trinh,
determined to regain control of the South, started a war that lasted,
with many interruptions to regain strength, more than fifty years.
They never reached Hue; after the failure of their last campaign in
1673, they gave up the attempt to reunify the country under their
authority. Both the Nguyen and the Trinh continued to pledge
loyalty to the powerless Le dynasty and to pay lip service to Vietnamese national unity, but they maintained, for the next hundred
years, their separate governments over the divided country.

A movement to reunify Vietnam, directed against both the Nguyen and the Trinh, started in 1772, but national unity was re-established only after thirty years of revolution and civil war, during which the fate of Vietnam began to be influenced by the West.

WESTERN PENETRATION INTO VIETNAM

It is impossible to fix an exact date for the beginning of the modern era of Western penetration into Vietnam. What seems certain is that a number of Portuguese adventurers explored the east coast of Indochina as early as 1516. Dominican missionaries are said to have visited Vietnam in 1527. The first military man, Captain Antonio da Faria, arrived in 1535. He established a Portuguese trading center at Faifo, some fifteen miles south of Danang. Although more Portuguese missionaries very likely arrived soon afterward, a regular though quite fragile mission was set up in Faifo only in 1596. When Jesuits, sitting idle in Portuguese Macao after being expelled from Japan, were allowed to enter Vietnam in 1615, the Faifo mission became permanent. Its Portuguese, Spanish, and Italian missionaries were joined during the same year by French Jesuits, among whom was Alexander of Rhodes, a Jesuit scholar from Avignon. This famous father of French missionary activity in Vietnam soon became the first French author on Vietnam.[24] He learned Vietnamese in six months and completed work on *quoc-ngu*, the transcription of the Vietnamese language into Latin characters, a task on which other missionaries had done preliminary work before Rhodes's arrival.

In spite of the war between North and South, Rhodes was able to go to Hanoi in 1627. He claims to have baptized 6,700 persons in two years, but he was expelled in 1630 by the Trinh, who began to resent the influence of foreigners on their subjects. Rhodes returned a few times clandestinely, but by 1645 he was definitely forbidden, by both the Trinh and the Nguyen, to re-enter the country.

French Catholic missionary work was from the beginning closely connected with simultaneous efforts to establish trade with Vietnam. In a book Rhodes published in Paris in 1653, written to enlist support for missionary work of people interested in trade with the Far East, he said that Vietnam was very rich. The country was fertile; it had quantities of pepper, many gold mines, and so much silk that silk was used for fishing lines and sailing cords. One of the French apostolic vicars for Vietnam, François Pallu, appointed by the Vatican to head the Vietnamese mission in 1658, was even more blunt in stating the need for cooperation between church and business. In a report written for the French East India Company, created in 1664 to advance trade with the East, Pallu wrote that the Company would have as many promoters of its aims as there would be bishops, priests, and believers in Vietnam.

But profitable business relations with Vietnam were difficult to establish. As long as the Trinh and Nguyen were interested in the acquisition of modern weapons, they tolerated missionary activity and accepted trade relations with the West—the Trinh chiefly with the Dutch, the Nguyen with the Portuguese. But when the wars between North and South came to an end in 1672, all of that changed. As a result, a trading center set up by the Dutch in Hanoi in 1637 did so poorly that it was closed in 1700. The British, who had come only in 1672, closed shop after only twenty-five years, in 1697. The first trading center of the French was opened as late as 1680. It met the same fate as those of the Dutch and English. After 1700, only the Portuguese managed to maintain a minimum of trade with Vietnam through their old establishment at Faifo.

In spite of these setbacks, the French continued their efforts to enter Vietnam during the entire eighteenth century, pursuing not only missionary work and trade, but also entertaining the idea of military intervention. Missionary progress, however, became more and more difficult. The mandarins, spiritual as well as political leaders of Vietnam, had long realized that their moral authority was being undermined by the teachings of Christianity. They began to persecute the missionaries and native Catholics, who constituted, then as now, about 10 per cent of the population. Successful trade was hampered by the poverty of the people, as one persistent Frenchman, Pierre Poivre, after visiting Vietnam several times, pointed out in 1750. The people had no part in any foreign trade, wrote one of the first eminent French historians of Vietnam, Charles Maybon, adding that without the people, solid and lasting commercial relations were impossible.

As the attitude of the rulers and mandarins of Vietnam became more and more anti-Western, more and more Frenchmen convinced themselves that only through military intervention could Vietnam become a base for French mercantile operations in the Far East. Typical of these men was one Count d'Estaing, who, in 1758, had the piratical notion of a brief military action against Hue for the purpose of robbing the imperial palace of all its gold and treasures. The project failed, but only nine years later, after some maturing of the count's colonialist concepts, he proposed an invasion of Tourane (Danang) with 3,000 soldiers as a first step toward making France the dominating Western power in the Far East. But France, unable after 1760 to defend its Indian possessions against the British, lacked both the spirit of enterprise and the material resources for such action.

CIVIL WAR AND REUNIFICATION

The prospects of the French took a sudden turn for the better toward the end of the eighteenth century, when another great French missionary, Pigneau de Béhaine, titular Bishop of Adran, managed to involve himself in the events that led to the reunification of Vietnam.

The revolution, which broke out in 1772 against both ruling houses of divided Vietnam, was led by three brothers, whose name in history, Tayson, was that of their native village. The Tayson succeeded in overthrowing the Southern regime of the Nguyen in

1777. With the exception of one nephew of the king named Nguyen Anh, all members of the royal family were killed. After conquering the Nguyen, the Tayson turned north against the Trinh. To defeat them, however, took more than ten years. During this time, Nguyen Anh, with the help of Cambodian mercenaries and Chinese pirates, reoccupied Saigon. But he lost it again to the Tayson in 1783. He was a refugee in Siam when the fall of Hanoi completed, for a brief period, the reunification of Vietnam by the Tayson. They abolished the Le dynasty in 1787. In 1788, China tried to exploit the crisis in Vietnam, but under the brilliant leadership of the youngest of the Tayson brothers, Nguyen Van Hue, the Chinese invaders were defeated. However, while the Tayson concentrated their strength to save Vietnam from falling again under Chinese domination, Nguyen Anh succeeded, with French help, in making himself once more master of Saigon and the entire South.

Ever since Nguyen Anh had first entered Saigon in 1778, Bishop Pigneau de Béhaine had been his constant companion and political adviser. The Bishop shared the prince's exile in Siam and, in 1786, agreed to go to Paris to seek French armed support for Nguyen Anh's project of wresting Vietnam from the Tayson. For French military help, Nguyen Anh was ready to grant France trade privileges and complete freedom of action for the missionaries. But on the eve of the French Revolution of 1789, the court of Louis XVI was neither willing nor able to send an expeditionary force to the Far East. The Bishop thereupon privately recruited sailors, soldiers, officers, and technicians from the French Navy and the French overseas possessions. Their military expertise was one of the reasons why Nguyen Anh eventually defeated the Tayson. However, to accomplish this took a series of long campaigns, lasting from 1788 to 1802. After Hue and Hanoi had fallen to Nguyen Anh's armies, the victor proclaimed himself emperor of the reunited country. He made Hue his capital and named his country Vietnam. Under the name of Gia Long, he became the founder of the last Vietnamese dynasty, the Nguyen, whose reign, nominal after 1883, ended with Bao Dai in 1955.[25]

STATE AND SOCIETY OF
PRECOLONIAL VIETNAM

During the last decade of the war against the Tayson, Nguyen Anh relied heavily on the advice, chiefly in military matters, of the French experts whom Pigneau de Béhaine had recruited for his royal friend. But when, as Emperor Gia Long, after exterminating the Tayson family he embarked on the task of consolidating his rule over his reunited country, he looked for guidance not to the West but to Vietnam's past. In his eyes and those of his successors, the past organization of the Vietnamese state and the principles on which Vietnamese society was built were valid also for the future. The basic features of the Vietnamese state had already been established by the Ly emperors in the eleventh century. They remained unchanged under the Tran and Le, and even usurpers and radical reformers like Ho Qui Ly never planned fundamental changes in state and society. Vietnam remained the centralized state founded in the eleventh century, headed by a monarch whose absolute powers were said to rest on a mandate of heaven. Gia Long actually reinforced this Chinese notion, as well as the strictly Confucian character of his reign. He left the hierarchy of civil and military mandarins untouched, and he continued to recruit all mandarins, from the highest at the court to the lowest in the local administration, through civil service examinations, taken after many years of study. This system favored the rich who could spend the time required for long studies, as well as the sons of mandarins, who constituted most of the candidates for the state-run civil service institutes. But the better rulers of all dynasties took repeated steps to enable exceptionally gifted children of peasants to enter the mandarinate. In periods of dynastic degeneration, public offices, a source of legal income, were sometimes for sale, but as a rule the road to positions of power remained scholarship, not wealth.

Gia Long, like all Vietnamese rulers before him, was not only the supreme lawmaker and head of all civil and military institutions but also chief justice in political, criminal, and civil cases, and it was

E

from him alone that the mandarins derived their equally broad authority. The concept of a division of powers was completely alien to precolonial Vietnam. Even public functions of a religious character were reserved to the emperor and the mandarins. An aristocracy with powers to oppose those of the emperor arose only in times of misrule and crisis. Titles of nobility were normally bestowed only as honors, declining in degree from generation to generation until they expired.

No economic development took place in precolonial Vietnam that might have altered the basis of royal and mandarin rule. Through the entire 900 years of independence prior to French rule, the country's economy was static, remaining exclusively agricultural. Some villages of artisans and fishermen existed, and there were also some people employed in mining, but apart from them, the mandarins, and the Buddhist monks, the great mass of the people were peasants, engaged almost exclusively in the cultivation of rice. Both national and international trade remained insignificant, since most villages and the country as a whole were economically self-sufficient. In times when the monarchy failed to check the growth of large landholdings, feudal ambition often threatened royal authority. But no property-owning middle class of merchants, contractors, lawyers, or owners of nonagricultural enterprises ever developed to compete with the mandarins for positions of power. And when, during the eighteenth and nineteenth centuries, the rise of such a class was no longer impossible, the emperors and mandarins, recognizing all economic innovation as a threat to their monopoly of power, made sure that the old economic basis of their rule remained intact. To safeguard their power against feudal ambitions, Gia Long and his successor Minh Mang even abolished all large landholdings during the first half of the nineteenth century. They insisted on the traditional concept according to which all land was owned by the emperor. In fact, it was only by imperial decree that the settlers of newly conquered territories had received their land in the new villages that had been founded during the centuries of the Vietnamese "March to the South."

Dynastic and mandarin rule was somewhat modified in two ways, which, if we cannot call them true elements of democracy, at least relieved the strict absolutism of the system to some degree. There was the Confucian concept of the family as the basic unit of civilized society, making submission to the authority of the head of the family the highest moral obligation of every Vietnamese. And there was the limited authority granted to the administration of the villages, at the gates of which, according to an over-optimistic saying, the power of the emperor ended. A council of notables, in principle elected but more often self-appointed, and consisting of the more prosperous or otherwise prominent citizens, such as retired mandarins and scholars, dealt with all purely local affairs, including law enforcement in the village, the levying of army and forced-labor recruits, and the assessment of taxes. Loyalty to the village was a deeply rooted sentiment in Vietnam and was regarded as the foremost duty of every citizen.

Compared with other countries, Asian and Western, precolonial Vietnam can be said to have been ruled competently by its great dynasties. In the opinion of D. G. E. Hall, an outstanding authority on the history of Southeast Asia, the administration of Vietnam was well in advance of any other native administration in Southeast Asia. But the rule of the mandarins had drawbacks also. Learned as these officials were, it remained a serious defect of their intellectual make-up that they looked for enlightenment only to the past and that their method of acquiring knowledge was largely restricted to learning classical literary and philosophical texts by heart. They were opposed to any innovation, not only technical and economic but also spiritual, and their hostility to change hardened precisely when the survival of an independent Vietnam required a systematic modernization of the country. The mandarins, ever since the arrival of the missionaries in the seventeenth century, and particularly during the first half of the nineteenth century, regarded innovation as a dangerous weapon of the West to undermine traditional Vietnamese society.

Contrary to the views of most French historians of Vietnam, Gia Long, too, shared these fears with the mandarins. He was grateful to

the individual Frenchmen who had helped him to become master of
Vietnam, and he kept several of them as advisers at his court.
(Pigneau de Béhaine had died in 1799, at the age of fifty-seven,
of dysentery contracted as early as 1788.) But Gia Long was a strict
Confucianist, and although the Catholics were not officially per-
secuted during his reign, he did not favor Christianity, as the mis-
sionaries in Vietnam knew only too well. His alleged attachment to
France was never put to the test. France, engaged during most of
Gia Long's rule in the Napoleonic wars, lacked the human and
material resources needed to pursue a systematic policy of establishing itself as a power in the Far East. Those who believed that Gia
Long was a friend of France became aware of his true sentiments
when he chose as his successor a man known for his strong anti-
Western and anti-Christian convictions. This was Minh Mang,
oldest son of Gia Long's first concubine. Minh Mang ruled Vietnam
from 1820 to 1841. He dismissed all remaining French advisers,
rejected all French proposals to establish diplomatic and trade relations with Vietnam, and made the persecution of missionaries and
Vietnamese Catholics the official policy. Between 1833 and 1838,
seven missionaries and an unknown number of Vietnamese Catholics
were executed, some for political reasons, having taken part in an
uprising against Minh Mang.

During the 1830's, France dropped its efforts to get into Vietnam
by diplomatic means, and from 1840 on Catholic propaganda
openly asked for French military intervention in favor of the per-
secuted missionaries. Minh Mang, fearing a possible French invasion
of his country, took steps to improve his relations with the West
during the last years of his reign, but the spokesmen for French
political Catholicism and the influential Society of Foreign Missions
insisted that his peace feelers be rejected. French militant Catholicism was convinced that the missionary cause in Vietnam could be
saved only through French military intervention.

Minh Mang's successor, Thieu Tri, who ruled Vietnam from
1841 to 1847, made desperate efforts to curb the activities of the

missionaries without antagonizing France. He ordered all missionaries expelled from Vietnam, but at the same time he made peace
overtures to French emissaries who arrived on warships at the harbor
of Tourane. When the missionaries refused to leave, he had some of
them condemned to death, but none was executed. French warships
frequently threatened the Vietnamese Government, often at the
initiative of naval commanders without clear orders from the French
Government, which still hesitated to embark on the course proposed
by missionary propaganda. One of the threats ended in a naval
bombardment of the harbor of Tourane in April, 1847, during
which hundreds of Vietnamese were killed within a few hours.
Another attack on Tourane by the French warship *Catinat* took
place in 1856, after the last full independent emperor of Vietnam,
Tu Duc, had ordered the execution of two French priests. By that
time, France, ruled by Napoleon III, was about ready to join the
Western powers in their policy of colonial conquests in the Far
East. It was during 1857 that missionary propaganda, strongly
supported by naval officers seeking military bases in Asia, succeeded
in persuading the government to prepare a military expedition
against Vietnam.[26]

4

The Century of Colonialism

F rench military intervention in Vietnam, which Napoleon III decided, in July, 1857, to undertake, was brought about less by missionary propaganda than by the rapid development of French industrial capitalism. It was during the 1850's that the colonialist concept of a need for overseas markets gained ground in France, together with the notion that a larger French share in Asian territories conquered by the West was required.

An old idea—to establish a French military base at Tourane—was taken up. The commander of the navy in the Far East, Admiral Rigault de Genouilly, long an advocate of French military action against Vietnam, was charged with the execution of the plan. Because of the Anglo-French war of 1857–58 against China, Genouilly was able to sail against Vietnam only in the summer of 1858. Fourteen vessels with 2,500 men on board—including the missionary

adviser, Monsignor Pellerin—arrived before Tourane on August
31, 1858. One day later, the harbor and the town of Tourane were
in French hands.

This initial success, however, proved deceptive. Vietnamese resistance prevented progress beyond Tourane. To make the court at Hue
agree to a French base at Tourane would have required storming the
capital. To reach Hue by land was out of the question, and since
Genouilly lacked the shallow-draft vessels needed to sail up the
Perfumed River to Hue, the Vietnamese capital and court remained
out of his reach. The French were stalled at Tourane even before
the rainy season, which in Central Vietnam starts in October, im-
mobilized them completely. Victims of tropical diseases soon out-
numbered battle casualties among the French forces.

Realizing that the scheme of getting a foothold in Vietnam could
not be accomplished at Tourane, Genouilly, after several despairing
months, decided to pursue it by attacking Saigon. Leaving a small
garrison behind with orders to hold Tourane, the French sailed south
on February 2, 1859. At Saigon too, the French were initially
successful. The conquest of the city was completed on February 17,
but progress beyond Saigon was as difficult to achieve as it had been
at Tourane. In the meantime, Vietnamese attacks seriously threatened
the French garrison at Tourane, forcing Genouilly to return there
in April, 1859. A French-Spanish garrison was left at the fortress of
Saigon. (The Spanish, who took part with troops from the Philippines during the first phase of the invasion of Vietnam, withdrew in
1862.) Completely discouraged, partly because the Catholic uprising in support of the French promised by missionary propaganda
did not materialize, Genouilly resigned his command and left for
Paris on October 31, 1859. Already in April, he had written to
Paris, in angry reference to his missionary advisers, that "the government had been deceived about the nature of this enterprise."
Genouilly's replacement, Admiral Page, arrived shortly before
Genouilly's departure, with orders to evacuate Tourane. The evacua-
tion was completed on March 22, 1860.[27]

The French opponents of this colonial enterprise began to denounce it as a complete fiasco, pointing out that a precarious position at Saigon was all that had been achieved two years after the French first sailed into the harbor of Tourane. Since the second phase of the Anglo-French war against China once more tied up the fleet, the action against Vietnam was completely stalled throughout 1860. Only in February, 1861, was the isolated garrison at Saigon relieved by a new expedition under the command of Admiral Charner. Reinforcements sent from China enabled Charner to extend French control over three provinces adjacent to Saigon by the end of June, 1861.

The mandarin officials refused to cooperate with the French, but their past opposition to modernization of their country had left Vietnam without any of the modern weapons that might have enabled them to block the invaders. Military deficiency, not lack of will to fight, forced the court of Hue, ruled since 1847 by Tu Duc, the last emperor of independent Vietnam, to sign away Saigon and the three lost provinces in the South in a peace treaty concluded with France in June, 1862. With this treaty, the court also granted the French the island of Poulo Condore, three open ports for trade with France, full freedom for all missionary activities, and a heavy financial indemnity. But the treaty was ratified only in April, 1863, after the French, thanks to fresh African and Algerian troops, had suppressed the first major Vietnamese uprising. Growing French military strength forced Tu Duc to accept also the loss of the Vietnamese provinces west of the Mekong, which the French Governor, Admiral de la Grandière, annexed four years later under the pretext of forestalling another anti-French uprising. From June, 1867, on, the entire South of Vietnam, called Cochinchina in the West, was in French hands.[28]

Cochinchina was for a long time the European name for all Vietnam, but the French, from the end of the eighteenth century on, used it only for the South. They called the North Tongking and the Center Annam but used Annam also for the country as a whole.

The Vietnamese never used these foreign designations. For them, the South was Nam Bo, the Center Trung Bo, and the North Bac Bo.

The eight years it had taken the French to extend control over all of Cochinchina were followed by sixteen years of diplomatic maneuver and two military operations before France, through the occupation of Annam and Tongking, was able to complete the conquest of Vietnam.

The first attempt to get into the Red River delta was made under the Admiral-Governor Dupré in 1873. This action, like many later ones by the colonial administration, was unauthorized by Paris. Dupré appointed Francis Garnier, a thirty-four-year-old explorer and adventurer, to lead the attempt to conquer Tongking. Garnier had shown, in a long and perilous expedition, that the Mekong River could not serve the French in Cochinchina as a trade route into Southwest China.[29] On the other hand, a French weapons dealer, Jean Dupuis, proved the Red River navigable by sailing, without Vietnamese permission, all the way up into the Chinese province of Yünnan. When the Vietnamese authorities stopped a second voyage by Dupuis, invoking old decrees forbidding foreign shipping on the Red River, Dupuis, who headed a band of two hundred mercenaries, barricaded himself in a suburb of Hanoi and appealed to Admiral Dupré for help. Dupré obtained the reluctant consent of the court of Hue for Garnier's expedition to Hanoi. The understanding was for Garnier to settle the conflict between Dupuis and the Hanoi authorities and to obtain, through negotiations, freedom of navigation on the Red River. Heading a small force of sixty soldiers and the crews of three ships, Garnier arrived in Hanoi in August, 1873. He immediately sided with Dupuis, which increased his armed force to more than three hundred men. After receiving more reinforcements from Saigon, he dropped diplomacy in favor of military action, bombarded and stormed the citadel of Hanoi, and, in the manner of a Roman general at the head of a conquered province, began to issue orders to the local

Vietnamese authorities. Through massive use of artillery, Garnier was able to extend his control over all important towns between Hanoi and the coast. But this first attempt to conquer the North collapsed when Garnier was killed in December, 1873, in a skirmish with Chinese pirates hired by the Vietnamese authorities.[30]

"To establish ourselves in this rich country bordering on China," Admiral Dupré had written to Paris in the spring of 1873, "is a question of life and death for the future of our rule in the Far East." But Paris did not share Dupré's opinion. In 1873, France had not yet recovered from its defeat in 1871 in the war with Prussia, and Paris refused to supply Dupré with the money and manpower needed to resume the conquest of Tongking. It was more important for France, the anticolonialist faction of the government asserted, to rebuild its strength in Europe than to undertake costly and doubtful colonial adventures.

It took ten more years of rapid economic progress before government and parliament were ready to admit that France must rejoin the race of the Western powers for colonial expansion. In April, 1882, the Saigon administration sent another expedition to Hanoi, this time with the consent of Paris. It consisted of 250 men under Captain Henri Rivière, who differed from Garnier only by being contemptuous of the Vietnamese people. Rivière acted exactly like Garnier, storming the citadel of Hanoi and many cities and fortified places in the North after receiving enough troops from Saigon. But when Rivière, in May, 1883, met the same fate as Garnier, the Chamber of Deputies immediately voted the credits for a strong expeditionary force to complete the conquest of Tongking. This force moved into the Red River delta in August, 1883. Simultaneously, the French fleet bombarded Hue. The court of Hue, no longer headed by Emperor Tu Duc, who had died three weeks earlier, decided to submit. The treaty extending French authority over the whole of Vietnam by making Tongking and Annam so-called protectorates of France was signed on August 25, 1883,

twenty-five years after the conquest of Vietnam had been started
with the ill-fated storming of Tourane.

Vietnam was conquered, but it took another fourteen years
of so-called pacification before the French could claim that their
control over the Vietnamese people was firmly established. As had
been the case in Cochinchina, where the French had to suppress
a general uprising in 1863, a broad movement of national resistance
developed in Annam in 1885. At the head of this insurrection,
supported by the court of Hue, was the fourteen-year-old Emperor
Ham Nghi. French control was quickly reduced to a few strong
points in Annam. The entire insurrection was suppressed only after
the capture of Ham Nghi three years later, in November, 1888.
Another armed rebellion broke out in 1893, led by the great scholar
Phan Dinh Phung, whose followers harassed the French for more
than two years all over Annam before the movement expired after
Phan Dinh Phung's death in 1895.

In Tongking too, the position of the French remained precarious
during this entire period. Local rebellions, many of them under
competent leadership, broke out both in the delta and in the mountainous regions of the North. In some provinces, French control
was suspended for several years. Pacification of Tongking can be
said to have been completed only in 1897, when the French offered
a treaty to the rebel leader De Tham (whose real name was Hoang
Hoa Tham), leaving their last great adversary in Tongking in control
of twenty villages for several more years.[31]

Four years earlier, in 1893, the French had annexed Laos.
As in the case of Cambodia, on which a protectorate had been
imposed in 1863, the French took Laos also under the pretext that
it had once been subject to Vietnamese control, although, in 1893,
Laos had long been controlled by Siam. The new conquest became
part of the so-called Indochinese Union, created by the French
in 1887 and consisting, after 1893, of Vietnam, Cambodia, and
Laos. It was headed by a French governor-general who resided at
Hanoi.

COLONIAL VIETNAM

Mandarin noncooperation and Vietnamese armed resistance no doubt retarded the establishment of a firm administration and prevented constructive steps toward a sound economic policy for Indochina during the first decade and a half of French rule. However, the chief reason why little or no political and economic progress was made was the inability of the French to determine how to administer their new possessions and how to develop them economically. Furthermore, the French in Cochinchina, who had done very well by exploiting the rich South of Vietnam for twenty years, vigorously opposed an all-Indochinese economic policy under a strong central administration. Hardly any progress, administrative or economic, was made even under competent administrators like Jean-Marie de Lanessan, appointed by Paris in 1891 and dismissed, at the request of businessmen and officials in Cochinchina, in 1894.

A drastic change came about only after the arrival of Governor-General Paul Doumer in 1897, the year pacification of Tongking was finally conpleted. Disregarding the protectorate status of Annam and Tongking, Doumer established direct French rule over the whole country, imposing his strict administration also on his obstinately separatist countrymen in Cochinchina. The court of Hue remained without a trace of real power, and the emperor, no less than the mandarins on all levels of the local administration, had to choose between serving the French and losing his position. Doumer staffed his administration with thousands of officials imported from France, using Vietnamese only in minor positions or to camouflage foreign rule to some extent with native names. The Vietnamese, even if employed higher up in the administration, were paid salaries amounting to only a fraction of what low-grade French officials earned. As late as 1930, after several more liberal governors-general had made concessions to local nationalist sentiment, all important administrative positions were still monopolized by Frenchmen.

Doumer was equally effective in determining, for almost the entire period of French rule, the basic economic and social policies pursued by the French in Vietnam. Preparing the country for systematic exploitation for the benefit of France, Doumer started the construction of railroads, highways, harbors, canals, bridges, and other public works, many of which, such as the railroads, were still not completed twenty years after Doumer had left Indochina in 1902. His aim was to make Vietnam, whose natural wealth he overestimated, a source of valuable raw materials and a tariff-protected market for goods of French industries. French investments went primarily into the exploitation of the country's natural resources for direct export, with rice leading, followed by coal, rare minerals, and later rubber as the main products. Neither Doumer nor any of his successors up to the eve of World War II was interested in promoting local industries. On the contrary, their development was consciously and strictly limited to the production of goods for direct local consumption. There were breweries, distilleries, sugar refineries, rice and paper mills, and some cement and glass factories. Most of these small industries were in Saigon, Hanoi, and Haiphong, except for Vietnam's greatest industrial establishment, a textile factory at Nam Dinh, which in the 1920's employed 6,000 workers. As late as 1930, the total number of workers employed in all industries and mines was 100,000. The guiding principle of French economic policy in Indochina was to put immediate profits before long-term economic considerations. Little or nothing of any profit was reinvested. Profits of the cotton mill at Nam Dinh reached 52 million francs annually in the 1920's, but production was not increased at all over the next twenty years. Colonial economic policy exploited but did not develop Vietnam.[32]

This is not to say that there was no economic progress at all. However, whatever progress was made was of benefit only to French private business and to a small class of large Vietnamese landowners created by the colonial regime. Neither the French state nor the French people ever shared in the profits that were made in Indochina. The treasury never recovered the sums spent during

the forty years of conquest and pacification, and the French con-
sumer paid as much for his rice or rubber products as did people
of countries without colonies.

In view of this, it cannot surprise us that the Vietnamese people,
direct objects of exploitation, gained nothing at all under the
colonial regime. On the contrary, there is much evidence that for the
majority life was harder in 1930 than it had been a hundred years
earlier. The mechanism by which this result was achieved, in the
face of a vast increase of riceland, can be found in the social policies
inaugurated by Doumer—land and taxation policies of the most
vicious kind, which were unfortunately upheld even by liberal
governors-general such as Paul Beau (1902–7), Albert Sarraut
(1911–13 and 1917–19), and Alexandre Varenne (1925–28).
It is a shocking revelation that, while the surface of riceland quad-
rupled between 1880 and 1930, the individual peasant's rice
consumption decreased during the same period, a loss not compen-
sated for by the consumption of other foods. The new lands made
available through vast irrigation works, chiefly in the Mekong
delta, were not distributed to the peasants who had too little, or
to the landless, but were either sold to the highest bidder or given
away, at nominal prices, to Vietnamese collaborators and French
speculators. This policy created the new class of large Vietnamese
landowners, who needed landless tenants to work their fields for
rents ranging up to 60 per cent of the crop, which left hardly enough
for the consumption of the tenants' families. But the higher the
rent, the more rice could be sold by the landlord at the Saigon
export market. Before World War II, Vietnam had become the third
largest rice exporter in the world (after Burma and Thailand). The
mounting export figures for rice, always cited by French apologists
of colonialism as proof of economic progress, were in fact due not
so much to the increase of cultivable land as to the mounting degree
of tenant exploitation.

Hardly better off than the tenants were the small landowning
peasants. After paying Chinese middlemen and French exporters,

their share of the price of rice at the Saigon export market was usually less than 15 per cent. These peasants continually ran into debt, and if they were unable to repay their debts in time, as was frequently the case, they lost their land to the big landowners who had lent them money at exorbitant interest rates. More and more small landholdings were thus wiped out. Toward the end of the colonial regime, the large landowners of Cochinchina, a mere 2.5 per cent of all landowners, owned 45 per cent of all land. The small peasants, 71 per cent of all landowners, together owned 15 per cent of the land. Somewhat different, but no less disastrous for the mass of the small peasants, were conditions in the greatly overpopulated Center and North of Vietnam.

But the landlords and other moneylenders, as well as the middle-men (mostly Chinese) between producer and exporter, were by no means the only ones guilty of peasant exploitation. After them came the colonial administration, collecting the outrageous taxes, direct and indirect, that Doumer had invented to finance his administration and his ambitious program of public works, consisting chiefly in highways used only by the French and underutilized railroads. There was, among many others, the iniquitous head tax: A peasant who made 50 piasters a year paid the same amount as a rich man who made 10,000. Then there was the tax on salt, a product everybody needed. Like opium and alcohol, the production and sale of salt was made a state monopoly. Heavy fines and high prison sentences were dealt out for unauthorized local production of salt, and the price of salt soon rose to more than ten times what it had been in precolonial Vietnam. Other ways of exploiting the people were the recruiting of forced labor for public works and the absence of any legal protection of the workers in the mines and rubber planta-tions, whose scandalous working conditions, low wages, and lack of medical care were frequently exposed in the French Chamber of Deputies. The same conditions also existed for the tens of thousands employed on the many public works projects. The economic infra-structure created by the colonial regime in Vietnam, inadequate as it was in every respect, was paid for by the taxes, the labor, the sweat, and the hunger of the Vietnamese people.

These illiberal and narrow-minded economic and social policies were of little benefit even to the small-scale French colonists, many of whom failed after years of struggle. The great profits were made by the larger French enterprises, most of which were controlled, if not actually owned, by the Bank of Indochina, which many French critics of colonial policy regarded as the colony's real government. Not only the French people but also most French industries were adversely affected by these antidevelopmental and exploitative policies. Although France between 1920 and 1939 had almost a 60 per cent share of all imports into Indochina, the colony never became an important market for French industry. The peasant masses, nearly 90 per cent of the population, remained too poor to become consumers of French goods. Only the 6,000 to 7,000 large Vietnamese landowners, some officials, and the French in Indochina were in the market for most goods imported from France.

The French have always insisted that they have done much for the Vietnamese in the fields of education and medical care, but their own statistics do not support this claim. As late as 1939, a mere 15 per cent of all children of school age received some kind of schooling. About 80 per cent of the population was illiterate after sixty years of French rule, in contrast to precolonial Vietnam, where 80 per cent of the people possessed some degree of literacy. A small number of Vietnamese children were accepted in the lycées created for the children of the French, but only one university, with fewer than 700 students, existed for the more than 20 million Vietnamese.

The record of the colonial regime is equally poor in regard to medical care, as one simple set of statistics proves. Colonial Vietnam had two physicians for every 100,000 people, compared with 25 in the Philippines and 76 in Japan.[33]

Only the hard-core colonialists were really surprised and em-

bittered when the Vietnamese, instead of being grateful for every-
thing France was said to have done for them and their country,
constantly searched for ways of opposing colonial policies and of
fighting to get rid of the colonial regime.

Two aspects of French colonial policy are especially important
for the direction taken by the Vietnamese people's resistance against
colonial rule, and for the political character of the nationalist movements. First of all, the absence of any kind of civil liberties, which
prevented the rise of democratically oriented groups and parties,
favored illegal organizations dominated by a revolutionary mental-
ity. Second, the exclusion of the Vietnamese from the modern sector
of the economy prevented the rise of a property-owning middle
class of a liberal and pro-capitalist outlook. Rubber plantations,
mines, and industrial enterprises, as well as local trade and the export-
import houses, were in foreign hands—French if the business was
substantial, Chinese on the lower levels. Capitalism, therefore,
appeared to the Vietnamese people, and especially to the educated
and politically conscious minority, as a product of foreign rule, to
be abolished together with colonialism. This, together with the
denial of democracy, explains not only the revolutionary character
of Vietnam's anticolonial movement but also why it was easy for so
many determined nationalists to embrace Communist ideas.

THE MOVEMENTS OF
NATIONAL LIBERATION

It is no exaggeration to say that Vietnamese resistance to colonialism started with the establishment of colonial rule—in Cochinchina
in the early 1860's, in Annam and Tongking after 1883. The main
characteristic of these first movements was their orientation toward
the past. Led by local mandarins, scholars, and high court officials
steeped in the ideas of precolonial Vietnam, the aim of all these
movements prior to 1900 was to re-establish the old imperial and
mandarin order. But these aspirations had little attraction for the

F

generations that reached maturity after 1900. As a consequence, the old resistance movements led by royalist mandarins, after being defeated militarily, were also dying politically.[34]

A new movement of national resistance, no longer dominated by ideas of the past, arose soon after the turn of the century. Its leader for almost two decades was the scholar Phan Boi Chau, a modern rationalist thinker violently opposed to French rule but ready to embrace the progressive political ideas, the science, and the technology of the West. Chau started out as a monarchist whose aim was a radically modernized Vietnam under a progressive emperor. In 1905, he went to Japan, followed in 1906 by Prince Cuong De, a direct descendant of Emperor Gia Long, whom Chau had chosen to head his modernized Vietnamese monarchy. Together with the prince, Chau founded the Association for the Modernization of Vietnam, thus reviving the true name of his country, which the French still called Annam, the name first applied to Vietnam by the Chinese in the third century A.D. For years, Chau nourished the illusion, mildly encouraged by some Japanese statesmen, of freeing Vietnam with Japanese help. Hundreds of young Vietnamese were brought to Japan by Chau's clandestine organization not only to study modern science but also to undergo training for illegal propaganda and terrorist action.[35]

Chau himself was a highly effective political propagandist. His many books and pamphlets were secretly distributed all over Vietnam, inspiring a variety of nationalist activities. In 1907, a group of Hanoi intellectuals opened the so-called Free School of Tongking, which immediately became a center of anti-French agitation. It was suppressed by the colonialist police after only a few months. Led by agents of Chau, mass demonstrations against the high taxes took place in many cities during 1908; inspired by nationalist sentiment, a movement of hair-cutters spread all over Vietnam, relieving the men of the long hair introduced by the Chinese. The French reacted by arresting thousands of demonstrators and hundreds of suspected organizers, condemning some to death and sending others to the island of Poulo Condore, which they had turned into a concentration camp for Vietnamese nationalists.

Chau lost his illusion that Japan would help Vietnam to gain national freedom in 1910, when he and Prince Cuong De, after Japan had received a loan from France, were expelled from Japan. In China, where revolution had broken out in Canton, Chau set up a republican government in 1912, with Prince Cuong De as president. He also united a number of nationalist groups in a League for the Restoration of Vietnam, but during a temporary setback of the Chinese revolution he was jailed by the local authorities at the request of the French. He was freed only in 1917, after the revolution had again triumphed in South China. Chau continued to work untiringly from exile, but his movement declined rapidly after the end of World War I. In 1925, French agents succeeded, allegedly through a Communist betrayal, in kidnaping Chau in Shanghai. He was brought to Vietnam and condemned to death, but Governor General Alexandre Varenne, a socialist, commuted the sentence to confinement for life at his house in Hue, where Chau died, almost forgotten, in 1940.[36]

Although no longer at its height after 1914, the Chau-inspired movement of national resistance nevertheless still manifested itself for several more years in many acts of terror, in demonstrations, and in brief local revolts: In 1916, nationalist sentiment prompted even the eighteen-year-old Emperor Duy Tan to head a rebellion against the French. The movement failed, and its participants were either executed or deported. The young emperor was exiled to Réunion, one of the French-held Mascarene islands in the Indian Ocean. He was replaced by the more pliant Khai Dinh, father of Bao Dai. Another uprising, staged by the indigenous garrison at Thai Nguyen in 1917, was also quickly and ruthlessly suppressed by French troops from Hanoi.

The continued decline of the revolutionary movement after 1920 led a number of prominent intellectuals, among them the

writer Pham Quynh, to seek political concessions through collaboration with the colonial regime, a movement supported only
by the class of large Vietnamese landowners and some civil servants.
Convinced of the harmlessness of these aspirations, the French
in 1923 permitted the founding of the Constitutionalist Party
of Cochinchina. It was led by Bui Quang Chieu, an agricultural
engineer and landowner who was also one of the first Vietnamese
to become a French citizen, and by the journalist Nguyen Phan
Long, a known proponent of collaboration with the French.

It was the expected total failure of these "reformist" efforts
that led to a revival of revolutionary activity, particularly in Annam
and Tongking, where not even the Constitutionalist Party was
allowed to operate. Among the new clandestine groups that arose
was the Vietnam Revolutionary Party, founded in 1924 in Annam,
where it existed a few years under several different names. More
important was the Vietnamese Nationalist Party (Viet Nam Quoc
Dan Dang, usually referred to as VNQDD), founded in 1927 in
Tongking and led by Nguyen Thai Hoc, a twenty-three-year-old
teacher. The core of the VNQDD was the nationalist intelligentsia.
The party organized terrorist action and penetrated the indigenous
garrisons, planning to oust the French through a military uprising.
But on the crucial date fixed for this event, the night of February 9
to 10, 1930, only the garrison of Yen Bay in Tongking rose. The
native troops killed their French officers but were defeated by
French troops one day later and summarily executed. In a wave of
repression that took hundreds of lives and sent thousands into concentration camps, Nguyen Thai Hoc and twelve other leaders of
his party were arrested and beheaded. The VNQDD, almost
destroyed in Vietnam, existed during the next fifteen years chiefly
as a group of exiles in China, supported by the Kuomintang.[37]

There had arisen, back in 1925, another clandestine group, the
Revolutionary League of the Youth of Vietnam, commonly referred
to as the Thanh Nien. It was founded by a man destined to become
the most prominent leader of the Vietnamese national revolution,

Nguyen Ai Quoc, better known by the last of his many pseudonyms, Ho Chi Minh, which he adopted in 1943. Ho Chi Minh's Thanh Nien, which soon absorbed the Vietnam Revolutionary Party and several other small groups in Annam, became the nucleus of the Communist Party of Indochina.

Ho Chi Minh had left Vietnam as a young seaman in 1912. He traveled widely before he settled in France in 1914. He joined the newly founded French Communist Party in 1920, spent a few years in Moscow, and was an agent of the Communist International in China when he founded the Thanh Nien in 1925. A very specific program for exploiting popular discontent, for organizing peasants and workers, and for instigating mass action soon made the Thanh Nien the most influential of all resistance groups. In 1930, Ho Chi Minh succeeded in uniting a number of competing Communist organizations in the Indochina Communist Party.[38]

Exploiting conditions of near starvation over wide regions of Annam, the Communists staged a general peasant uprising in May, 1930. Local "soviet" administrations were set up in several provinces of Annam, and many Vietnamese officials in the service of the French, as well as large landowners, were killed during these events. Full French control over Annam was re-established only in the spring of 1931. A committee headed by the French author Romain Rolland reported that, during 1930 and 1931, 699 Vietnamese were executed without trial, 83 sentenced to death, 546 imprisoned for life, and about 3,000 others arrested and put into concentration camps. Vietnamese nationalist sources estimated that the number of persons killed in the fighting during 1930 and 1931 exceeded 10,000.[39] A jubilant governor-general, Pierre Pasquier, told his countrymen that, "as a force capable of acting against public order, Communism has disappeared" from Vietnam.

Only a few years later, it became evident that Pasquier must have made his statement on the basis of faulty information. Replenishing its losses with cadres trained in Russia and China, the Communist Party quickly recovered from the defeats the entire nationalist movement had suffered in 1930 and 1931. By 1936, when the government of the Popular Front in France granted some civil rights to the people of the French colonies, the Communist Party apparatus, fully reconstituted, was able to extend its influence over intellectuals, workers, and peasants by skillfully exploiting all existing opportunities for the creation of legal "front" organizations. In Tongking, for instance, the Party operated under the cover of an Indochinese Democratic Front, led by two as yet unknown Communists, the future Prime Minister Pham Van Dong and the future General Vo Nguyen Giap. In Saigon, the Communists lost much of their following to two Trotskyite groups, and their influence elsewhere in Cochinchina was somewhat checked by the progress of two so-called religious-political sects, the Cao Dai, which had been founded in 1926, and the Hoa Hao, which arose only in 1938.[40] Nevertheless, at the outbreak of World War II, when all political freedoms were again abolished, the unified Communist Party, alone of all revolutionary groups in command of a well-indoctrinated and disciplined following, was by far the strongest faction of the entire nationalist movement.

TOWARD NATIONAL INDEPENDENCE

Between September, 1940, and the Japanese surrender in August, 1945, Vietnam was in fact, if not formally, a Japanese possession, administered by the French for the benefit of Japan. The French administration was headed during this period by Admiral Jean Decoux, whom the German-dominated Vichy government, after the fall of France, had appointed in July, 1940. On September 22, 1940, an agreement was concluded in Hanoi between Decoux and the Japanese general Nishihara, which permitted Japan to station 6,000 men north of the Red River and 25,000 more over the whole of Indochina. The Japanese were also allowed to use all major Vietnamese airports. The Japanese Army moved into Indochina not only to prevent further shipments of arms via Tongking to the Chinese fighting the Japanese invaders of their country but also to make Indochina the most important base for their intended future military operations in Southeast Asia.[41]

Although Vietnam was ruthlessly exploited by the Japanese occupation forces, the French continued to cooperate with them until the Japanese ousted Decoux's administration on March 9, 1945.[42] Many French officials were arrested, and the French troops stationed in Indochina were disarmed and interned. The Japanese took this step to prevent the French from turning against them in the hour of Japan's approaching defeat. Some of the French in Indochina, afraid of being punished by the victorious Allies for their cooperation with the Japanese, secretly plotted such a move.

After the French were ousted, Bao Dai, the last French-appointed emperor of Vietnam, was allowed to proclaim the independence of Vietnam on March 11, 1945. On April 17, Bao Dai appointed the scholar Tran Trong Kim to form a national government. It consisted of French-educated intellectuals, all highly patriotic men, but it was a cabinet without either the resources or the power to govern. The Japanese continued to remain in command.

Under the persecution of both the French administration and the Japanese, the activities of the Vietnamese nationalists during the first years of the war were almost entirely restricted to propaganda by word of mouth and the distribution of some clandestinely printed papers. The religious-political sects in Cochinchina were an exception. Some of the sect leaders displayed pro-Japanese sentiments, not so much under the illusion of gaining Japanese support for Vietnamese independence as in order to enjoy Japanese protection against persecution by the French.

However, the men who emerged as the true leaders of the national revolution, Communists and anti-Communists, were almost without exception exiles in South China during the war. There, Ho Chi Minh, in May, 1941, founded the Viet Nam Doc Lap Dong Minh, subsequently known as the Viet Minh, a "united front" of nationalist groups, some non-Communist but in favor of "united action," others merely created by Communist organizers to broaden their control over all sectors of the population. The anti-Communist leaders in China knew that the Viet Minh was under firm Communist direction, and so did the Chinese Nationalists. Under their patronage, a Vietnamese nationalist counterfront to the Viet Minh, the Dong Minh Hoi, was created in China in 1942, and Ho Chi Minh was imprisoned on orders of Chiang Kai-shek. Led by the utterly incompetent old nationalist Nguyen Hai Than, in exile since 1906, the Dong Minh Hoi turned out to be useless for the Allies, who needed intelligence about the Japanese in Indochina and help in leading pilots downed by the Japanese out of Vietnam. The Allies, Chinese as well as American, soon found out that only the Viet Minh was able to offer them these services. Under the direction of Vo Nguyen Giap, the Viet Minh, since 1943, had built up a tight organization of political agents and guerrillas in northern Tongking, which soon controlled larger parts of the provinces of Thai Nguyen and Bac Kan than the French. For obvious political reasons, the Viet Minh leaders were eager to make themselves useful to the Allies, who in turn needed the information the Viet Minh could supply. Ho Chi Minh was released from prison in 1943, and, although he became the only Viet Minh member of the Dong Minh Hoi, he was soon directing its entire activities, with financial assistance from the Allies. He even received some weapons from the American Office of Strategic Services (OSS), to be used for anti-Japanese work inside Vietnam. Needless to say, Ho Chi Minh used whatever support he received exclusively to promote the cause of the Viet Minh. He himself entered Vietnam in October, 1944.[43] After the Japanese had ousted the French administration, the Communists, always ready to change their slogans for the sake of short-term expediency, proclaimed that the Japanese had become "the only enemy of the Vietnamese revolution." Three days after the Japanese surrender on August 10, 1945, the Viet Minh, from a conference held in the "free zone" they controlled in Tongking, ordered a general uprising against the Japanese.

The Viet Minh at this time was the only nationalist group whose leaders were in the country. Heading the only well-organized polit-ical and military movement in Vietnam, the Viet Minh, after the surrender of Japan, was able in the second half of August, 1945, to take power in Hanoi without meeting any serious opposition. The Bao Dai—appointed government at Hue, which had vegetated as an unwilling tool of the Japanese, resigned on August 22, and Bao Dai himself, a pleasure-seeker but still a Vietnamese patriot, abdicated on August 25 in favor of the emerging Viet Minh regime in Hanoi. In Cochinchina, a "Provisional Executive Committee of South Vietnam," installed in Saigon and composed of the religious-political sects, the Trotskyites, the Communists, and several other nationalist groups, also placed itself under the authority of the Hanoi regime on August 25. Ho Chi Minh formed his first government on August 29. On September 2, he proclaimed the independence of Vietnam before an enthusiastic mass of 500,000 people gathered in Hanoi for the occasion. Vietnam, so it seemed, was finally free, not only of Japanese but also of French rule, again an independent nation under a government headed and controlled by the Communist-led Viet Minh.[44]

5

Independence and War

THE FRENCH RETURN TO VIETNAM

After proclaiming the country's independence and founding the Democratic Republic of Vietnam, the Viet Minh, from the beginning of September, 1945, on, worked feverishly to extend its control from the North over the Center and the South of Vietnam. With the exception of the religious-political sects and a few minor groups, none of which dared openly to reject the Hanoi regime, the Viet Minh met little opposition and soon headed the provisional local administrations in Hue and Saigon. Millions of non-Communist nationalists, like Bao Dai and his royal delegate in Hanoi, were carried away by their enthusiasm for national independence, accomplished under the leadership of the Viet Minh.[45] In early September, the anti-Communist nationalists—apart from the sects in Cochinchina—lacked both political organization and military units.

78

Their most prominent leaders entered Vietnam only with the Chinese armies of occupation, weeks after the Viet Minh had begun to establish itself in most towns and villages all over Vietnam. There can be no doubt that, had it not been for outside military interference, Vietnam, independent and again unified, would have become a Communist-controlled state in the fall of 1945.

It is impossible to overemphasize the importance of certain unique aspects in the political evolution of Vietnam immediately after World War II. The Communists were able to seize power in Hanoi without meeting opposition, and they were on the way to gaining control of the entire country a few weeks later—all of this more than four years before the victory of Communism in China. Unlike the Communists in Poland, Rumania, Bulgaria, and Hungary, the Vietnamese Communists were capable of gaining power without the presence of a single soldier of a foreign Communist army in their country. They did not have to be given a few positions in a so-called coalition regime, which they would then abuse to gain total control of the government. Like Tito in Yugoslavia, Ho Chi Minh directed a political and military movement more powerful than that of his combined enemies, even had these been organized and united. To obstruct the rise of a Communist Vietnam required political and military interference from abroad. British help enabled the French to start this interference as early as September, 1945.

Because French and, later, American propaganda has claimed for more than two decades that Western interference in Indochina was necessary to stop the spread of Communism in Asia, it is necessary at this point to investigate the true reasons for the determination of the French to reoccupy Vietnam.

As early as March, 1945, the French Government, headed by de Gaulle, who at that time probably had never heard of the Viet Minh, announced to the people of Indochina that French colonial rule over their countries would be re-established after the defeat of the Japanese.[46] De Gaulle knew that President Roosevelt had opposed the return of the French to Indochina, but at the end of the war Roosevelt was dead and his successor Truman was not sufficiently concerned about the fate of Indochina to take a firm stand. At the Potsdam conference in July and August, 1945, where the Allies divided the spoils of victory, the French, with strong British support, obtained what they rightly considered a free hand in Indochina. The French were dismayed when the Chinese under Chiang Kai-shek, who were opposed to French reoccupation of Indochina, were charged with disarming the Japanese in the Northern half of Vietnam. The French regarded the Chinese as an obstacle to their project of returning to Indochina. But in August, 1945, not even the best-informed Frenchman, Jean Sainteny, saw Vietnam threatend by Communism.[47] Indeed, the military intervention of the French in Indochina was not directed against Communism, which before 1947 was hardly even mentioned as a danger: It was the result of a decision, made by the French long before the appearance of the Viet Minh in Hanoi, to re-establish their colonial regime and thus was clearly directed against the independence of Vietnam, Cambodia, and Laos.

It was a great relief for the French that the British, on whom they could count to help them get back into Indochina quickly, were given the task of disarming the Japanese in the South. The first British troops arrived in Saigon on September 12, 1945, under the command of General Douglas D. Gracey. Fortunately for the French, Gracey, a man politically several decades behind his time, saw nothing wrong with colonialism. But he was shocked by the disorder that the progress of the national revolution was creating in Saigon. Contrary to formal instruction from his superior, Admiral Louis Mountbatten, Gracey interfered in the internal affairs of Vietnam by taking action to curb the activities of all nationalist groups.[48] He gave orders to have the Vietnamese disarmed but, at the same time, released and rearmed the French troops whom the Japanese had interned. This enabled the French, after the arrival of their first troops from abroad on September 21, to oust, two days later, the Vietnamese authorities established by the Committee of the South and to occupy all important public buildings in Saigon. The Committee of the South, whose chairman was the Communist Tran Van Giau, ordered a general strike and a counterattack against the French. But more and more French troops arrived on British and American ships, turning Saigon, after several weeks of Vietnamese resistance, into a French-occupied town.[49] General Leclerc, the commander of the French Army, was able to embark, at the end of October, on a campaign to return the entire South of Vietnam to French control. But it took the French, with an army of 35,000 men, more than three months before they could claim to have reestablished their administration in the South. The truth is that by February, 1946, the French controlled no more than the major towns and highways, while their rule in the countryside was effectively contested by the guerrillas whom the Committee of the South, encouraged by Hanoi, had mobilized all over Cochinchina and southern Annam.[50]

It cannot be sufficiently emphasized that, in 1945 and 1946, the French never described their actions in the South as being directed against Communism. Indeed, much of the resistance they met at this time was offered by the anti-Communist sects. The actions of the French were naked colonial aggression, openly directed against the common goal of *all* nationalists: the independence of Vietnam. This French attitude applied also to the North. Vastly underestimating the popular support enjoyed by the Viet Minh, the French regarded the Chinese armies of occupation as a greater obstacle to the extension of their control over the North than the Communist-led Hanoi government. Nobody, of course, foresaw that, in launching the reconquest of Vietnam in September, 1945, the French had initiated a war that would still rage over all of Indochina twenty-five years later.

HO CHI MINH BETWEEN THE CHINESE
AND THE FRENCH

Up to March, 1946, it was indeed not the Hanoi government that prevented the extension of French control over the North but the presence of the Chinese armies of occupation. It was therefore quite obvious that the French were no threat to the existence of the Hanoi regime so long as the Chinese remained in the country. On the other hand, no such simple explanation exists for the fact that Ho Chi Minh survived the threat that the presence of the Chinese Nationalist armies constituted for the continuation of his regime.

Various reasons have been advanced to explain why the Chinese generals abstained from replacing the government of Ho Chi Minh, whom they knew to be a Communist, with a government of the nationalist parties whose leaders the Chinese armies had brought back to Vietnam. Such action could not have been interpreted as being directed against the independence of Vietnam, which the Chinese Nationalists in principle favored. If no such action was taken, the reason can only be that the Chinese generals were afraid to risk the consequences of interference by force in the course the national revolution had taken before their arrival. These generals knew very well that the Vietnamese people regarded the Chinese occupation as a national misfortune. Plunder by Chinese soldiers and stealing by their officers had made the occupation a bitter experience for the entire people and a disaster for the country's economy.[51] Hatred of the Chinese was one reason why their protégés, the anti-Communist nationalists, failed to gain popular support.

The removal of the Viet Minh, whose popularity was evident, and the setting up of a government of pro-Chinese nationalists would risk a possible general uprising under Viet Minh leadership. The Chinese, who accused the French of aggression, could ill afford to create conditions in the North similar to those the French had created in the South. That is surely one of the reasons why they limited themselves to putting pressure on the Viet Minh in favor of the VNQDD and Dong Minh Hoi, demanding no more than a share for their protégés in the existing government. However, they may have tolerated Ho Chi Minh because his government made no effort to curb the activities through which some of the Chinese military and political leaders in the North enriched themselves, activities that the Chinese could not have pursued if they had cast the Viet Minh out of power and into a campaign of sabotage and guerrilla warfare against the hated foreign occupation.

In a series of dexterous maneuvers, Ho Chi Minh complied formally with most of the Chinese demands without losing a single position of real power to his largely incompetent adversaries. To appease the Chinese, Ho Chi Minh even dissolved the Communist Party in November, 1945. He made an offer to the leaders of the VNQDD and Dong Minh Hoi to join his government, under conditions, however, that the nationalists declined, fearing to be merely trapped into giving up their Chinese-protected anti—Viet Minh activities. In December, 1945, Ho Chi Minh announced the holding of elections, which aroused violent protests among his nationalist opponents. He accepted a Chinese request that the nationalists be guaranteed 70 of 380 seats in the National Assembly, for which, as everybody knew, the pro-Chinese parties, lacking organization and popular support, could not have obtained the necessary votes. The elections, held on January 6, 1946, produced the expected overwhelming victory for the Viet Minh.[52]

Ho Chi Minh needed little Chinese pressure when he agreed, on February 24, to form a government consisting of four members of the Viet Minh, four anti—Viet Minh nationalists, and four so-called neutrals, the latter being secret allies of the Viet Minh. He knew already that the Chinese Government at Chungking was about to make a deal with the French that would lead to the departure of the Chinese troops. What was true of the generals of the occupation army, who were warlord types with no genuine concern for their Vietnamese protégés, was true also for the Chinese Nationalists under Chiang Kai-shek: They were not really interested in promoting Vietnamese independence. In a treaty concluded on February 28, 1946, France gave up all its possessions and prerogatives in China, gaining China's agreement to let French troops relieve the Chinese occupation armies between March 1 and 15, 1946.[53] It is safe to assume that, in anticipation of this treaty, the Chinese generals in Vietnam had long since decided that the question of how to deal with the firmly entrenched Viet Minh was, after all, a problem for the French. Toward the end of February, 1946, it grieved these men as little to leave the pro-Chinese nationalists to the mercy of the Viet Minh as it had grieved the Chungking government to leave the cause of Vietnamese independence to the mercy of the French.

Long before the Nationalist Chinese betrayed the cause of Vietnamese freedom, Ho Chi Minh had realized that French determination to recolonize Indochina, not Chinese sympathy for his opponents, would sooner or later threaten the survival of his regime. He also knew that the French, since they were not fighting Communism but Vietnamese independence, would disregard the fact that, in the government he had formed on February 24, the Viet Minh were a minority and that prominent Communists like Vo Nguyen Giap were excluded from it. Ho Chi Minh had formed this government for purely internal reasons. Since the beginning of January, 1946, Ho Chi Minh had been conducting secret talks with Jean Sainteny, the chief representative of the French in Hanoi. The French entered these negotiations because they knew that their own military strength was still insufficient for a successful campaign in the North. The Viet Minh regime, six months after its inception, commanded a respectable number of regular army units and many thousand members of an armed militia. Besides, much French military power was engaged in operations against the guerrillas in the South. Rather than force their way into the North at the risk of having to deal with armed resistance all over the country, the French decided to recognize the Hanoi regime if Ho Chi Minh agreed to the stationing of French troops in the North.

The reasons why Hanoi, too, preferred a deal with the French to armed resistance are not hard to understand. The military strength of the Viet Minh could not have prevented a French invasion of the North. All the Viet Minh could hope for was a long war of resistance, led chiefly by guerrillas, with no hope of outside help. China was still ruled by Chiang Kai-shek, the Soviet Union was far away, and Stalin showed no interest whatever in Vietnam. On the other hand, the hopes in Hanoi that France, moving politically to the left, might break with the policy of colonial conquest within a year or two seemed not at all unreasonable. These hopes certainly justified the experiment of a temporary compromise, if this would spare the people the agonies of a long war. However, Ho Chi Minh knew that a treaty permitting the French to station troops in the North would be the first truly unpopular step taken by the Viet Minh. This, not Chinese pressure, was the main reason why he formed his government of February 24. Being in the government, the anti–Viet Minh nationalists would have to share responsibility for a decision that Ho Chi Minh knew would come as a shock to the entire people.

The Franco-Vietnamese agreement concluded between Ho Chi Minh and Sainteny on March 6, 1946, stipulated that 15,000 French troops and 10,000 Vietnamese under French command would be stationed in Hanoi, Haiphong, and several other cities of the North; in return for this concession, France recognized the Hanoi regime as the government of a "Free State" within the French Union, as the French euphemistically described their colonial empire. The French also promised to permit a referendum in the South through which Cochinchina could be reunited with Vietnam, and, even more surprising, they agreed to withdraw their forces from Vietnam within five years.[54]

The reaction of the anti–Viet Minh nationalists to the March agreement corroborated both their deficient political intelligence and their lack of national responsibility. Instead of rallying behind their government at this critical moment in the nation's history,

G

they accused Ho Chi Minh of having surrendered to the French. Believing that they had a chance to gain popular support, they started a vicious anti-French propaganda campaign in which they depicted the Viet Minh as traitors to the cause of national independence. But as often happens during a crisis in a nation's history, the people had more political sense than the men who tried to lead them. The people understood the motives that had led Ho Chi Minh to compromise with the French, and they remained faithful to the leader whom they had begun to identify with the cause of national liberation. The French, who entered Hanoi on March 18 with a massive display of tanks and other heavy weapons, were still far from claiming that it was their mission to stop Communism in Vietnam. On the contrary, a Communist willing to enter into the compromise which French weakness at the time still required, was preferable at the head of the so-called Free State of Vietnam to an anti-Communist whose program consisted in claiming that his nationalism was more anti-French than that of the Viet Minh. The result of these witless tactics was that the French cooperated for several months with the Viet Minh in the elimination of the anti-Communist nationalists from the political life of North Vietnam. Unprotected by the Chinese occupation forces, who gradually left after March, 1946, The VNQDD and Dong Minh Hoi were systematically suppressed in Hanoi and driven from the several provinces where the Chinese armies had maintained them in power. Before the end of 1946, many of their leaders were again exiles in China.[55]

TOWARD THE FIRST INDOCHINA WAR

The Viet Minh leaders remained undeceived by the cooperation the French had extended to them in suppressing the pro-Chinese nationalist parties. They knew such joint actions were temporary and that it would be absurd to expect them to reduce the differences that existed between Paris and Hanoi in regard to ultimate aims.

The French, no matter what their tactics were in the spring of 1946, worked consistently for the re-establishment of colonial rule, while the Viet Minh in the end would not settle for anything short of total independence.

The real intentions of the French were made quite clear by the new High Commissioner for Indochina, Admiral Thierry d'Argenlieu, appointed by de Gaulle in October, 1945. D'Argenlieu was a rigid colonialist, as impervious to other people's aspirations that interfered with French aims as de Gaulle himself, who, in August, 1946, stated that France, without its overseas territories, would be in danger of losing its status as a great power. Although a stout Christian—d'Argenlieu had spent some time in a monastery before World War II—the new High Commissioner nevertheless believed that only force could re-establish French rule throughout Vietnam. He opposed Sainteny's negotiations with Ho Chi Minh and even criticized General Leclerc, who knew that he lacked the forces needed for a successful campaign in the North and therefore endorsed the idea of returning to Hanoi through an agreement with the Viet Minh regime.[56] At the risk of being recalled by Paris, d'Argenlieu, to the delight of the French in Vietnam, publicly denounced the March agreement, insisting that none of its stipulations was binding for the French in the South. Emissaries sent by Hanoi to arrange a cease-fire in the South were arrested, and no steps were taken toward unification of Vietnam through a referendum in Cochinchina.[57] On the contrary, from March, 1946, on, d'Argenlieu prepared a move designed to render the division of Vietnam permanent by making Cochinchina a separate "state." Under the correct assumption that Paris would in the end support his policy, d'Argenlieu, far from taking steps to realize the promise of eventual independence, did all he could to retract the concessions France had made in the March agreement.

Because of this attitude, a first conference held in Dalat in April, 1946, between the French and delegates from Hanoi produced only mutual accusations and, among the extremists on both sides, the conviction that the conflict between French colonial aims and Vietnamese national aspirations would have to be settled by force.

Circumstantial evidence makes it almost certain that Ho Chi Minh was then still far from accepting this pessimistic conclusion. He urged the French Government to allow the Franco-Vietnamese talks provided for in the March agreement to be held in Paris, where he knew the atmosphere would be more favorable to his cause than in French-occupied South Vietnam. Paris agreed, but whatever hopes for progress Ho Chi Minh may have had when he left for France on May 30, 1946, could hardly have survived the news he received on June 1, the day chosen by d'Argenlieu, without authorization from Paris, to proclaim Cochinchina an Autonomous Republic. Ho Chi Minh vainly expected Paris to repudiate this action.[58]

In order to keep the Vietnamese delegates, of whom many were non–Viet Minh nationalists, away from Paris, the conference was held in Fontainebleau. Because of a French Government crisis, it did not start until five weeks after the arrival of the Vietnamese delegation. The conference, which lasted from July 6 to September 9, broke up without agreement on any of the disputed issues, merely confirming the views of d'Argenlieu and the pessimists among the Vietnamese leaders that the time for the use of force was rapidly approaching.

Because Ho Chi Minh wanted not to let it appear that a final break had occurred in Franco-Vietnamese relations, he agreed to a so-called *modus vivendi*, which he concluded with the Minister of Overseas France, the Socialist Marius Moutet, on September 14. The *modus vivendi* granted a number of French requests designed to improve the French position in the North, in return for which Ho Chi Minh received nothing, not even a repetition of the empty promises France had made in March. It is idle to speculate why Ho Chi Minh signed such a document. To say that he wanted to gain a few more months to improve Hanoi's military position does not necessarily contradict the view that he was still hoping to avoid the threatening war.[59]

But this war could have been avoided only if the French, too, had thought it advisable to continue a policy of compromise. This was no longer the case, as a growing number of provocative actions by the French demonstrated. A French attempt on November 20, 1946, to take away, unilaterally, customs control from the Hanoi regime led to a major clash between French and Vietnamese troops in Haiphong. The French military decided to use this incident "to teach the Vietnamese a lesson," as d'Argenlieu put it. When the Vietnamese failed to comply with an ultimatum requesting that their troops evacuate Haiphong, the French attacked on November 23, killing, by their own admission, at least 6,000 civilians in a naval bombardment of the city's Vietnamese quarters.[60]

Frantic negotiations between Ho Chi Minh and Sainteny during the next three weeks only revealed that the French were determined, at the risk of a war whose nature and duration they disastrously misjudged, to establish their undivided rule also over the North. When they demanded that the Viet Minh militia at Hanoi be disarmed, Ho Chi Minh and his colleagues realized that they had to choose between armed resistance and capitulation. They decided to fight. Their attempt, on December 19, 1946, to overwhelm the French troops at Hanoi is commonly regarded as the beginning of the First Indochina War. In reality, the war merely spread at this time over the whole of Vietnam, since it had started fifteen months earlier in the South, on September 23, 1945, the day the French ousted the Vietnamese authorities in Saigon.

FRENCH POLITICAL DECEIT AND MILITARY FAILURE

A great deal has been written about the Indochina War and its political background, but the meaningful facts can be related quickly. It took the French almost two months to gain control of the major cities and highways of the North and Center of Vietnam. Hue was taken on February 7, 1947, Nam Dinh on February 11, and

resistance in Hanoi ceased on February 19, exactly two months
after the start of hostilities.[61] This slow pace of the French reconquest of the North was an ominous portent of future difficulties,
since the Hanoi regime had not yet engaged, and would not for
several years, its regular army divisions, which had been withdrawn
into the mountainous far north of the country before December 19.
For almost four years, the Viet Minh opposed the French only with
locally recruited guerrillas and some larger regional military units,
controlling, at night if not always by day, most of the countryside,
as they still did, after more than one year of fighting, over much of
the South. Viet Minh control of the country beyond the cities and
highways was possible only because the guerrillas enjoyed not only
the sympathy but also the active support of the vast majority of the
people.

A change in this pattern of the war came about only in 1950,
some time after the victory of Communism in China. An ample
supply of weapons from the Chinese Communists enabled the Viet
Minh to take the offensive, engaging for the first time the divisions
of regular troops kept in reserve and augmented in numbers for
several years. During September and October, 1950, the French
were forced out of all their strategically important positions along
the Chinese border, and they were even in danger of losing Hanoi
before an able commander, Jean de Lattre de Tassigny, re-established
their position during 1951. But only one year later, the French
were again on the defensive, in spite of the aid France had begun to
receive from the United States. American policy, determined by the
obsessive fear of Communism in Asia, had begun to consider the
Viet Minh a tool of Soviet and Communist Chinese expansion,
disregarding the fact that the Russians had ignored the Vietnamese
struggle for independence and that the Vietnamese Communists
had come to power four years before the victory of Communism
in China.[62]

The French, always as confident of a military solution in their
favor as the Americans would be fifteen and twenty years later,

were for a long time blind to the real political cause of the conflict, which was the determination of the Vietnamese people, including all incorruptible anti-Communist leaders, to fight for the unity and independence of Vietnam. Not until the summer of 1947 did the French, under the new High Commissioner Émile Bollaert, begin to act as if they understood that independence, not Communism, was the basic issue in Vietnam. But they dealt with the political issue of the conflict in a devious way. Because the French were un-willing to relinquish their position of colonial domination, their political maneuvers were bound to fail. After two years of negoti-ations and some success in enlisting corruptible or politically gullible national leaders, the French succeeded, with financial inducements and brazen political promises, in placing former Emperor Bao Dai at the head of a nominally independent Vietnam. This fraudulent way of dealing with the basic political issues was denounced by all firm nationalists, Communists and anti-Communists alike. Men like the conservative Catholic leader Ngo Dinh Diem could not be persuaded to lend their names to this deception. More than ever, independence remained linked to the struggle against the French conducted by the Viet Minh. Not even the excessive brutality with which the Communists treated their enemies lost them the sympathy of the people, who by and large believed that anyone murdered by the Viet Minh must be, as was sometimes the case, a traitor to the national cause. There existed, after 1949, a French-controlled Vietnamese state, which was eventually also allowed to have its own national army. But as a military instrument against the Viet Minh, this army was as ineffective militarily as the Bao Dai govern-ment was useless politically as a tool of the French.[63]

Before the end of 1953, most of Tongking, with the exception of the lower Red River delta, was in the hands of the Viet Minh, as was much of Laos. Viet Minh guerrillas and regional forces also held sway over wide areas along the coast of Vietnam, the Central Highlands, and the Mekong delta. When, in February, 1954, a strong French garrison was encircled at Dien Bien

Phu in northwestern Tongking, the military position of the French became truly desperate. The prospect of certain defeat at Dien Bien Phu strengthened the opposition against the war in France. The men in the National Assembly and the government who favored a compromise solution of the conflict suddenly were able to sway French opinion. But only after the U.S. Congress, strongly advised by the British statesmen Churchill and Eden, had refused American military intervention to save the French at Dien Bien Phu was France at last ready to negotiate a political settlement of the Indochina War.[64]

ONCE AGAIN TWO VIETNAMS

At a conference in Geneva, already in session when Dien Bien Phu fell to the Viet Minh under General Vo Nguyen Giap on May 6, 1954, an agreement was concluded, and signed on July 21, 1954, by the commanders of the French and Viet Minh armies that brought the First Indochina War to an end. The Geneva Agreement provided for a cease-fire, for the execution of which the country was divided at the Seventeenth Parallel into two military zones. The Viet Minh forces were to retreat north of the dividing line, the French and the State of Vietnam troops to the south of it. The agreement also permitted anyone, within a stipulated period, to move from one zone into the other.[65]

The Viet Minh leaders, having been convinced before they went to Geneva that total victory was within their reach, must have had compelling reasons for accepting a solution that limited their control to the Northern half of the country. These reasons were the justifiable expectation of an early extension of their rule over the entire country and some Soviet as well as Chinese pressure. In fact, a Final Declaration of the Geneva Conference made it clear that the Seventeenth Parallel was not to be regarded as a border between two permanently separated Vietnamese states. It was to be no more than a temporary dividing line between the country's two "military zones," which all-Vietnamese elections in July, 1956, were supposed to abolish. The Final Declaration containing this important provision was endorsed by the participants of the Geneva Conference, which comprised delegations from France, the Hanoi and the Bao Dai regimes, the United Kingdom, the United States, the Soviet Union and the People's Republic of China. But even the U.S. delegate, who expressed reservations against the Final Declaration, assured the conference that Washington "would refrain from the threat or use of force to disturb the agreement."

Assured of soon becoming masters of the entire country, the Communists started the reconstruction of the war-ravaged North. Great sacrifices were imposed on the people. All sectors of the economy were socialized. With financial and technical assistance from China, the Soviet Union, and other Communist states, Hanoi embarked on a vast program of forced industrialization. A brutally conducted campaign to collectivize agriculture and some periods of food shortages led to brief local revolts in 1956, but these were only transitory obstacles in the North's steady economic progress between 1955 and 1965. Political stability was underlined by the fact that the leadership in Hanoi consisted in 1965 of the same people who had made the revolution twenty years earlier.[66]

In contrast to the North, South Vietnam went through several periods of severe political crisis and changes of leadership between 1954 and 1965. On June 16, 1954, the Chief of the State of Vietnam, former emperor Bao Dai, asked the Catholic leader Ngo Dinh Diem to form a new government for the South.[67] It took Diem a whole year to master, against tremendous odds, the political chaos prevailing in the South after the defeat of the French and to build, with profuse aid from the United States, a stable anti-Communist regime in Saigon. To achieve this goal, Diem had to eliminate the pro-French leadership of the army, defeat and disarm the religious-political sects, and abolish their French-created local political autonomy. He also mastered the tremendous task of resettling more than half a million refugees from the North, most of them Catholic peasants. In October, 1955, after a prolonged conflict with the Chief of State residing in France, Diem ousted Bao Dai in a government-controlled referendum that elected Diem President of the Republic of Vietnam.

After surprising the world with these achievements, Diem's capacity for constructive leadership was apparently exhausted. Unlike the better monarchs of the dynasties of precolonial Vietnam, Diem failed to understand the vital importance of a sound agricultural policy for Vietnam. The crying need for a radical land reform was not met. Diem's program of protection for tenants and land distribution, decreed in 1956, was not only far too limited in scope but was also effectively sabotaged by the many members of the landlord class holding important positions in the administration. Instead of combating, with American aid, the social causes that had led so many of his countrymen to follow the Viet Minh, Diem preferred to fight the Communists with totalitarian methods of propaganda combined with police and army terror against regions known to be still Viet Minh—controlled. More than 80 per cent of the total American aid went into building up the army, sustaining the administration, and financing the many secret services and security forces that the regime needed to keep itself in power against mounting popular discontent. The Buddhists, leaders and followers, complained about the many advantages given to the Catholics, whom Diem soon had reason to regard as his only reliable supporters. The highly political intellectual elite was incensed by the denial of basic civil liberties and the arrest of anyone who dared openly to criticize the regime, often men of known anti-Communist convictions. Eventually, even formerly loyal members of the civil service, as well as officers and generals of the army, began to oppose Diem's dictatorship. What enraged these men was the arbitrary method of promotion and punishment, dealt out, in disregard of merit, solely on the basis of demonstrated loyalty to the President and to the members of his family, the only ones with a share in power. Elections were conducted so as to produce the results customarily achieved in totalitarian states. A secret party, formed and led autocratically by the President's brother Ngo Dinh Nhu, engaged chiefly in spying on and intimidating officials, army officers, and prominent private citizens suspected of lacking enthusiasm for the regime. Even early American supporters of Diem, regarding him as an answer to the attraction Ho Chi Minh exercised on the Vietnamese people, finally had to admit that the Saigon regime was a repressive and politically ineffective police state.[68]

General discontent and the lack of meaningful social and economic progress favored the insurrection that the Communists started a year after Diem's refusal to hold the elections of July, 1956, provided for in the Geneva Agreement. Politically guided and materially supported by Hanoi, this insurrection engulfed the entire South in a civil war after 1960. Diem's Communist enemies came close to victory toward the end of 1963, when the embittered leadership of the army decided to take action. The hated regime was overthrown on November 1, 1963, by a military coup, and Diem and his brother Nhu were assassinated by the leaders of the rebellion.[69]

6

The Second Indochina War

POLITICAL INSTABILITY IN THE SOUTH

The generals who had overthrown Ngo Dinh Diem formed a provisional government headed by former Vice President Nguyen Ngoc Tho as Prime Minister. On November 7, 1963, the new regime of South Vietnam was recognized by Washington, which had secretly welcomed and supported the coup against Diem. On January 6, 1964, this provisional government was replaced by a military triumvirate with General Duong Van Minh as Chief of State.

It was characteristic of the political instability prevailing in South Vietnam after the fall of Diem that this new regime, too, turned out to be highly provisional. It was overthrown on January 30 in another coup, led by General Nguyen Khanh, who assumed almost dictatorial powers as Prime Minister, keeping for a brief time General Duong Van Minh as titular Chief of State. But political instability continued to plague the Saigon regime under General Khanh and all through 1964. No fewer than nine changes of government took place before the final ouster of General Khanh by an Armed Forces Council on February 21, 1965. A civilian government under Prime Minister Phan Huy Quat was tolerated by the military for four months, but on June 18, 1965, Air Vice Marshal Nguyen Cao Ky openly assumed power as Prime Minister, with General Nguyen Van Thieu as Chief of State.

The main cause of continued political instability under the changing Saigon regimes was that in 1964 the South Vietnamese armed forces remained just as incapable of dealing successfully with the Communist-led insurrection as they had been under Diem. The crying need for drastic political and social reforms, which might have created popular support for Saigon, was not recognized by either the new civilian or the military leaders. Land reform remained a dead issue. Landlords were still permitted to extract illegal rents of 60 per cent and more from their tenants, pushing them into maintaining their sympathy for, if not actual support of, the Vietcong, as the forces that tried to overthrow the Saigon regime were called.

While there have been more than a dozen governments in power between 1954 and 1970 in South Vietnam, in the North, the same men who made the revolution in August, 1945, were still at the helm twenty-five years later. Not even the death of Ho Chi Minh on September 3, 1969, shook the unity of the Hanoi leadership or produced serious conflicts of succession.

THE COURSE OF U.S. INTERVENTION

The period between the fall of Diem and the rise of Ky was fateful, for both South and North Vietnam, for the effect the threatening collapse of the Saigon regime had on the evolution of U.S. policy in Vietnam. Throughout 1964, President Johnson and his military and civilian advisers prepared two policies that led to the sharp escalation of fighting in 1965. The first, the bombing of the North, began in February, and the second, the dispatch of American combat troops, started in March, thus opening what has been called the Second Indochina War.[70]

Prior to the fall of Diem and the assassination of President Kennedy, the number of U.S. military personnel had been limited to 16,500 so-called advisers to the South Vietnamese armed forces. By the end of 1964, U.S. military strength in South Vietnam had been raised to 23,300, still considered to be there only in an advisory capacity. The first regular troops, two battalions of Marines, were dispatched to the harbor city of Danang on March 6, 1965; these were limited to defensive security duties. The U.S. troop level stood now at 27,000. But not only was this level from then on raised in quick steps—it stood at 45,500 in May and at 148,000 in October—but the role of the U.S. troops also changed, from advising the Vietnamese and defensive duties to an active and aggressive combat role in so-called search-and-destroy operations. These operations, which increased as U.S. troop strength rose to more than 500,000 early in 1968, were conducted with an abundant use of artillery and air power, causing not only widespread material destruction but also millions of refugees and many hundred thousand civilian casualties. Like the divided and politically incompetent leadership in Saigon, Washington, too, had succumbed to the fallacy that maintaining a military dictatorship and killing more and more Vietcong, at whatever cost to the country and the people, were the best ways of dealing successfully with the insurrection. A great many promises for a better and freer way of life for the people of South Vietnam were constantly made, but the political and social reforms that might have immunized the peasants, students, and intellectuals against Communist propaganda and attached them to an anti-Communist regime were never undertaken.[71] Nor was there any recognition, either in Saigon or in Washington, that this neglect of reforms was the main reason why the ranks of the Vietcong and the influence of its political arm, the National Liberation Front (NLF), kept growing from year to year. From a fighting strength of less than 20,000 in 1960, the Vietcong had risen to an estimated strength of 140,000 when the American military build-up started in the spring of 1965, and to nearly 250,000 by June, 1967, although Vietcong losses were said to have been more than 150,000 between 1965 and 1967.

The build-up of the American ground forces was accompanied by the air war against the North, which, after an isolated attack in August, 1964, was started on February 7, 1965, and was conducted, under the code name Rolling Thunder, on a sustained basis from March 2 on. The raid on August 4, 1964, against North Vietnamese oil depots and patrol boat bases was in reply to an attack by North Vietnamese PT boats on the American destroyer *Maddox* in the Gulf of Tongking; the bombing on February 7, 1965, of a North Vietnamese military training center at Donghoi was in response to an attack by the Vietcong on the U.S. military advisory compound at Pleiku in the Central Highlands; but the sustained bombing raids ordered by President Johnson on February 13 and directed against targets that the Joint Chiefs of Staff had already selected as early as April, 1964, were undertaken in order to force Hanoi to cease supporting the Vietcong and to agree to a negotiated settlement of the war on American and South Vietnamese terms.

On March 7, President Johnson authorized the use of napalm in the bombing of the North and the extension of the attacks to nonmilitary objects, especially industries. The extent of damage caused by a monthly average of 60,000 tons of bombs dropped on North Vietnam was considerable, as was the number of casualties, which, according to a Central Intelligence Agency (CIA) report had reached 36,000 by January, 1967, of which an estimated 80 per cent were civilians.[72] But the objectives of the air war—to cripple the North's economy, to interdict infiltration of Northern troops and supplies into the South, and to force Hanoi to accept peace on American terms—were not achieved.

CIVIL WAR OR
AGGRESSION FROM THE NORTH?

It has been a constant theme of American and South Vietnamese propaganda to describe the fighting in the South as the result of systematic infiltration of troops and supplies from the North, and the bombing and intervention of U.S. ground forces in the South as necessary steps to prevent Hanoi's aggression from succeeding. This version was dogmatically maintained in spite of the American intelligence community's view that "the war began largely as a rebellion in the South against the increasingly oppressive and corrupt regime of Ngo Dinh Diem." The people "who took up arms were South Vietnamese and the causes for which they fought were by no means contrived in the North."[73] On the contrary, the former Viet Minh who began in 1957 to respond with violence to Diem's attempts to wipe them out acted against orders from Hanoi. North Vietnam, concentrating all its efforts on achieving economic progress in both agriculture and industry, expected the unification of the country to come about in one of two ways: either through the all-Vietnamese elections provided for in the Geneva Agreement or through the collapse of the Diem regime. Of the terror acts committed at the beginning of the insurrection in 1957, American intelligence officers in Saigon said that "there is only sparse evidence that North Vietnam was directing, or was capable of directing, that violence."[74] No more than 4,500 infiltrators made the trip from North to South during 1959 and 1960. However: "From later interrogations of captured infiltrators United States intelligence officers learned that until 1964, almost all the infiltrators were native Southerners who went to the North in 1954."[75]

No less contrary to the facts was the assertion of American propaganda that the air raids against the North and the dispatch of combat troops to the South were a direct response to the infiltration of regular army units from North Vietnam. Testifying before the Senate Foreign Relations Committee on January 28, 1966, Secretary of State Dean Rusk said that the 325th Division of the North Vietnamese Army had come down to South Vietnam between November, 1964, and January, 1965. The true figures and dates for the beginning of infiltration of regular army units from the North had been given already on August 27, 1965, by Secretary of Defense Robert McNamara, who stated that the first North Vietnamese units, not a division but a battalion of 400 to 500 men, entered the South during March, 1965, four weeks after the start of the American air raids against the North.

Total enemy strength, almost exclusively recruited in the South, was 140,000 at that time. To add to this figure a mere 400 to 500 Northerners, even if they had arrived before March, 1965, could hardly have prompted Washington to take the first steps toward a nearly total Americanization of the Vietnamese war. The real reasons for U.S. intervention in the spring of 1965 were the growing strength of the Southern insurrection and the political decline of the Saigon regime. It was to prevent the collapse of this regime under Vietcong military pressure that the bombing of the North and the massive intervention with U.S. combat troops in the South were begun.[76] Only two years later, in the spring of 1967, did the number of North Vietnamese regular troops in the South reach 50,000, one-tenth of the total American and other non-Vietnamese allied troops in the South, whose number at that time stood at 500,000. The air war had not prevented the steady flow of men and supplies from the North, and half a million allied and 600,000 South Vietnamese troops had not succeeded in reducing the fighting strength of the Vietcong. What had started as a civil war in the South had become an international confrontation between the United States and the Saigon regime on one side and the Hanoi regime and its allies in the South on the other. The enemy's Tet offensive of February, 1968, proved that, after three years of fighting, the Vietcong, supported by the North Vietnamese, while unable to achieve a military victory

H

over the Saigon and U.S. forces, was still as far from being defeated as it had been when U.S. intervention on a large scale started early in 1961.

SAIGON'S POLITICAL EVOLUTION

The Ky-Thieu government, which had installed itself in June, 1965, was supported only by the military and was no more popular than any of its predecessors since General Khanh had taken power on January 30, 1964. It met widespread opposition, which in March, 1966, broke out in turbulent demonstrations, particularly in the cities of Hue and Danang. Brutal force by the army and police was employed to suppress this opposition, which, like the movement against Diem in 1963, was led chiefly by spokesmen of the Buddhists. The Buddhists increasingly opposed the policy of seeking an end to the war through a military victory and instead advocated a political compromise with the enemy—the reason why their voice had to be silenced and their opposition suppressed.

As under Diem, rule by force was accompanied by widespread corruption in the administration and the army, from the top to the bottom. Corruption, it was reported by informed American observers, was taking no less than 40 per cent of U.S. aid to South Vietnam.[77] The beneficiaries of this corruption were not only contractors, high administrators, landowners, generals, and intermediary agents between business and government, but also lower officials in the administration who extracted bribes from any citizen for whatever service he may have needed and had a right to receive. Those rich enough were able to get exemption from military service for their sons or permission for them to study abroad, for which sums as high as $10,000 were paid.[78]

Although Washington was doubtless concerned about this corruption and expecially about the theft of much of the money the United States poured into South Vietnam, there was little it could do as long as its policy required the support of a regime not subject to public criticism and institutions of control. In fact, more than by corruption, Washington was troubled by the openly dictatorial aspects of a regime that was being defended against Communism in the name of democracy and freedom. Some of the military regime's dictatorial features had to be hidden behind pseudo-democratic trimmings to bridge the gap between rhetoric and political reality.

In the face of growing opposition against their methods and aims, the men in power in Saigon felt the same need. They were therefore not disinclined to apply some of the modern political techniques, especially that of manipulating elections, with which dictatorships frequently try to camouflage their true political nature. A Constitutional Assembly was elected in September, 1966, and elections for a President and a Senate were held a year later, on the basis of a constitution that, in so far as it did not remain entirely on paper, was tailored in all important respects to the needs of the ruling military clique, whose exercise of uncontrolled power remained untouched.

The elections of September, 1967, could look like an act of democracy only to someone unaware of the true conditions under which they were held. Freedom of the press was denied by keeping the sale of newsprint a government monopoly. Even so, four Saigon newspapers were suppressed during the election campaign. There was no freedom of assembly, and electioneering was severely limited by administrative ordinance. Candidates considered too dangerous, such as General Duong Van Minh, were barred from running; because he was suspected of "neutralism"—a slanderous term applied to anyone in favor of a political solution of the conflict— Minh was forbidden to return from exile in Bangkok. Also forbidden to run was Au Truong Thanh, a former member of Ky's cabinet who had converted to a policy of seeking peace through compromise. Several thousand Buddhists arrested in March, 1966, remained in jail, and the Buddhist slate for the Senate election was rejected under some flimsy pretext.

Shocking proofs of election frauds were produced by all the defeated civilian candidates after the presidential elections, in which, in spite of all precautions and manipulations, the military candidates for President and Vice President, Thieu and Ky, were elected with only 35 per cent of the vote. Buddhists and students demonstrated against this fraudulent election result, and a commission of the Constitutional Assembly actually decided, by a vote of 16 to 2, that the election should be annulled. But under direct and open government and police pressure, the full Assembly, by a vote of 58 to 43, decided, in the presence of the chief of police, to accept the election result. Significantly, Truong Dinh Dzu, the civilian candidate who had dared to advocate a peaceful solution of the conflict, came in second with 17 per cent of the vote. He was thrown into jail soon afterward and had still not been released four years later when new presidential elections were due.

The new elections held on October 3, 1971, were made ludicrous by the fact that there was only one candidate for President, Nguyen Van Thieu. Thieu's two chief rivals, former Vice President Ky, who had fallen out with Thieu, and General Duong Van Minh, recognizing that Thieu's control of the government apparatus made his victory a foregone conclusion, refused to run and called the whole procedure a "farce." Thanks to his own carefully conducted administrative preparation and in the absence of any other candidate, Thieu naturally was "re-elected," but nobody believed the government claim that 87.7 per cent of the registered voters had turned out and that Thieu had received 91.5 per cent of all the votes cast in his one-man race.[79] Washington, which had acclaimed the 1967 elections as a "major step forward," was obviously embarrassed by an "election" that differed very little from similar fraudulent exercises under Communist or other totalitarian regimes.

In view of this political regression, it is no surprise that corruption on all levels of the administration remained as flagrant as it had been in 1967. This was confirmed on February 8, 1972, by Vice President Tran Van Huong, who must surely have known the facts, in an indignant denunciation of this cancer in the social body of South Vietnam.

THE MILITARY STALEMATE

Early in 1968, after almost three years of heavy air raids on the North and with U.S. troop strength nearing half a million men, the military situation remained what it had become during 1966, when the threat of a Vietcong–North Vietnamese victory on the battlefield had been contained: a stalemate that neither side was able to break.

That the air war against the North, although constantly increased in intensity, would not turn the tide in favor of the South had been recognized by Secretary of Defense McNamara already in November, 1966, when he said in a memorandum to President Johnson that bombing the North "had no significant impact on the war in South Vietnam."[80] But with a few exceptions, the responsible men in Washington and Saigon, civilian as well as military, could not see a fact that, if they had recognized it, would have obliged them to admit that their aim of a military solution of the conflict in favor of the South was impossible to achieve. The commander of the American troops in Vietnam, General William C. Westmoreland, expressed unrestrained optimism in his assessment of the military situation at the end of 1967, delivered to President Johnson on January 27, 1968.

Only four days later this optimism was shattered, for all willing to see, by the great Tet offensive of the Vietcong during which, in addition to Saigon, Danang, and Hue, thirty-four provincial and sixty-four district towns were attacked, proving that no part of the country and none of the towns considered secure were effectively controlled by the Saigon regime.

The Tet offensive of February, 1968, in which the North Vietnamese troops acted only as auxiliary forces to the Vietcong, came as a shock both to the American military and to President Johnson. In a reaction close to panic, General Westmoreland, supported by the Joint Chiefs of Staff, requested an additional 206,000 troops, apparently considered necessary to re-establish a military situation that, in his mistaken judgment, had been excellent at the end of 1967. In order to justify this request, the generals painted a sober but obviously much truer picture of the military situation than the one they had offered prior to the Tet offensive. A report written on February 28 by General Earl G. Wheeler, the Chairman of the Joint Chiefs of Staff, after a visit to Vietnam described the alleged big losses of the enemy—40,000 killed, 3,000 captured, and 5,000 disabled—but concluded that the enemy's "recovery is likely to be rapid" and that "his determination appears to be unshaken." General Wheeler even admitted that the Vietcong had regained the initia-tive, that it was "operating with relative freedom in the country side," and that it had driven the Saigon army back into "a de-fensive posture around the towns and cities." Pacification, General Wheeler said, "has been set back badly," and the refugee population increased by 470,000 people. "The people of South Vietnam," the report concluded, "were handed a psychological blow, par-ticularly in urban areas where the feeling of security had been strong."[81]

In Saigon, the fighting lasted almost two weeks; the old imperial city of Hue in Central Vietnam was retaken, after being nearly razed by artillery and bombing raids, only at the end of February; and of Bentre in the Mekong delta, which suffered the same fate as Hue, an American officer said, "we had to destroy the city in order to save it." Countless noncombatants lost their lives during those weeks. Vietnamese and American sources later claimed that the Vietcong had murdered several thousand people in Hue, but little was said about the fact that "nearly four thousand civilians were killed in Hue, most of them by American air and artillery attacks."[82]

The Vietcong may have lost forty thousand men, although this figure was "disputed by some [American] intelligence officials," but since vast rural and many urban areas had for some time fallen back under their control, they succeeded in fully replacing their losses within several weeks.[83] South Vietnamese and American propaganda called the Tet offensive a fiasco for the enemy, since he had failed to achieve his objective, which allegedly was the overthrow of the Saigon regime. But, for most Americans and Vietnamese, and apparently also for President Johnson, the Tet offensive proved that the Vietcong, in spite of the bombing of the North and the "search-and-destroy" operations in the South, was stronger in February, 1968, than it had been at the beginning of massive U.S. military intervention. Only blind optimists could fail to see that a military stalemate would henceforth be the main feature of the Vietnamese war.

In a study by the Pentagon Office for Systems Analysis made after the Tet offensive, this fact was recognized, even if not publicly admitted. "Despite a massive influx of 500,000 U.S. troops [and] 1.2 million tons of bombs a year . . . our control of the countryside and the defense of the urban areas are now essentially at pre-August 1965 levels."[84]

CASUALTIES, COSTS, AND DESTRUCTION

It takes little imagination to realize what the amount of destruction and the rate of civilian casualties in the Second Indochina War must be if one learns that the United States had dropped, on South Vietnam alone, 3.6 million tons of bombs as of December, 1971. This compares with a total tonnage of 2 million dropped in World War II and of 1 million in the Korean War. For the whole of former French Indochina—South and North Vietnam, Cambodia, and Laos—the total tonnage of bombs dropped between 1964 and the end of 1971 was 6.2 million. This means that the U.S. has dropped 300 pounds of bombs for every man, woman, and child in Indochina, and 22 tons of bombs for every square mile. Enormous craters dot the landscape in many regions covering dozens of square miles. Hundreds of villages were totally destroyed by bombs and napalm, forests over vast areas defoliated, making the land infertile for years, and crops destroyed, with little or no consideration for the needs of the people, merely on suspicion that some of the crop might benefit the enemy.

What this meant in terms of human suffering becomes evident in the statistics of civilians killed, wounded, and displaced. The U.S. Senate Subcommittee on Refugees, under Senator Edward M. Kennedy, has put the number of civilians killed during the war as of August, 1971, at 335,000, the number of wounded at 740,000, and the total number of people made refugees at more than 5 million. There were at this time also 1 million refugees in Laos and 1.6 million in Cambodia. It was reported that the bombing in Laos was responsible for 75 per cent of the refugees.[85] The Saigon Ministry of Health estimated that about 40 per cent of all civilian casualties were due to bombing and shelling. The monthly civilian toll has risen from 95,000 to 130,000 during the period from 1968 to 1971.[86]

The rise of the refugee population in South Vietnam was partly due also to the past American policy of removing from countless villages, for strategic reasons, the entire population, and of putting these unfortunate people in what were called refugee camps or relocation centers. More often than not, these camps were to begin with nothing but empty fields surrounded by barbed wire.[87] Senator Kennedy, who visited some of these camps, found that thousands of persons there were "literally starving to death."[88] The callous attitude toward human suffering is well illustrated by the fact, also revealed by Senator Kennedy, that total expenditures for the entire refugee program, as of 1967, were less per year than what the United States spent on the war in half a day.[89]

Civilian casualties caused by the bombing of North Vietnam were held relatively low by the Hanoi government's policy of evacuating the people from the most endangered cities and by the building of air raid shelters all over the country. But destruction

was widespread, especially in the industrial suburbs of Hanoi and
Haiphong, in the steel-producing center of Thai Nguyen, and in
many smaller cities with industries, such as Nam Dinh, the center of
North Vietnam's textile industry, which was almost completely
destroyed.[90] However, as the Defense Intelligence Agency had
pointed out already in November, 1965, "the primarily rural nature
of the area permits continued functioning of the subsistence economy," which meant, as a study of the Institute of Defense Analysis
put it, that the bombing of the North "had no measurable direct
effect" on Hanoi's capability to supply its troops and the Vietcong
in the South.[91]

High as the number of American casualties in the war is so far—
45,627 killed and 302,896 wounded as of December 31, 1971—
it is small in comparison with the number of Vietnamese killed and
wounded since the beginning of the armed struggle. In addition to
the 335,000 killed and 740,000 wounded civilians, the South
Vietnamese army has suffered 137,000 killed and 300,000
wounded. The number of killed Vietcong and North Vietnamese has
been estimated at 788,000 toward the end of 1971—a figure often
disputed and no doubt containing, as Secretary McNamara put it,
"unarmed porters or bystanders"[92]—in other words, civilian casualties created by the disregard for Vietnamese lives displayed no less
by the Americans than by both Vietnamese sides. The number of
civilians killed in Laos has been estimated at 100,000, and in
Cambodia at tens of thousands. Not counting the battle casualties in
Laos and Cambodia and the civilian casualties in North Vietnam,
this adds up to a figure of 1.4 million Vietnamese killed and probably at least three times as many wounded.

This vast destruction of the land and killing of the people of
Indochina was costly for the United States not only in American
lives but also in money, to a degree that staggers the imagination.
The sum of 150 billion dollars spent on the war as of December,
1971, must be regarded as a conservative figure. More than 33
billion of this total was devoured by the air war, in which, by the

end of 1971, more than 8,000 aircraft of various kinds had been lost. Some of these, such as the F-4 jet, cost as much as $2.5 million each.

By relating the expenses for the war to the number of alleged enemies killed, some critics have established that it cost the United States more than $300,000 to kill one Vietcong. One single amphibious operation in the Mekong delta was said to have cost $16 million. A total of twenty-one enemies were killed in this operation, which meant that it cost no less than $800,000 to kill one Vietcong.[93]

Secretary of Defense McNamara, secretly opposed to the war since 1966 but still defending it publicly, was undoubtedly right when he wrote, in a memorandum to the President of May 19, 1967: "The picture of the world's greatest superpower killing or seriously injuring 1,000 non-combatants a week, while trying to pound a tiny backward nation into submission on an issue whose merits are hotly disputed, is not a pretty one."[94]

A TURNING POINT IN THE WAR

The Tet offensive of February, 1968, had profound repercussions in the United States. President Johnson himself was obviously deeply shaken in his belief that a favorable military solution of the conflict could somehow be achieved. After some hesitation and a great deal of discussion with advisers inside and outside the administration, the President decided to reject the request for 206,000 more troops for Vietnam, to recall General Westmoreland, to restrict the bombing in the North to below the Twentieth Parallel if Hanoi agreed to negotiate, and, more significant still, not to seek re-election. There can be no doubt that these decisions not only were made in response to good advice but were brought about also by the upsurge of popular opposition to the war that the Tet offensive had engendered.

To Washington's great surprise (and to the distress of some

officials), Hanoi, on April 3, replied positively to President Johnson's proposal by offering to meet with U.S. representatives "with
a view to determining with the American side the unconditional
cessation of the U.S. bombing raids and all other acts of war against
the Democratic Republic of Vietnam so that talks may start."[95] The
first session of formal negotiations between American and North
Vietnamese representatives was held in Paris on May 13, 1968.

Little need be said about all previous attempts by Washington
to get Hanoi to the conference table and why these had been rejected
by Hanoi. All earlier peace proposals had offered no concessions nor
any prospects for compromise but had simply marked publicly un-
stated conditions for peace that were nothing less than a demand for
the enemy's surrender.[96] Under Secretary of State George W. Ball,
one of the earliest opponents of Johnson's Vietnam policy, in a
memorandum to the President on July 1, 1965, stated the case
succinctly: "So far we have not given the other side a reason to
believe that there is *any* flexibility in our negotiations approach. And
the other side has been unwilling to accept what *in their terms* is
complete capitulation."[97] Hanoi agreed to the Paris peace talks not
only in response to the bombing restriction but also because of the
prospect of obtaining a complete halt of all bombing raids on the
North once negotiations started. The North Vietnamese leaders were
not mistaken in this expectation. On October 31, 1968, President
Johnson announced that the United States would cease "all air,
naval, and artillery bombardments of North Vietnam" as of
November 1.

Since the core of the Vietnamese problem after 1954 has been the
struggle of the Communists and their allies for free participation in
the political life of South Vietnam, Washington, once the principle
of a peaceful settlement was accepted, could hardly oppose the idea
that the parties at conflict in the South be included in peace negoti-
ation.[98] However, the leaders of the Saigon regime were firmly
opposed to admitting representatives of the National Liberation
Front to the conference table. On August 27, 1968, President Thieu

stated categorically that South Vietnam would not talk to the NLF. He even dissociated himself from President Johnson's decision to halt the bombing of the North, and when a tentative agreement was reached between Washington and Hanoi to widen the Paris talks by including the Saigon regime and the NLF as of November 6, President Thieu said on November 2 that his government would not accept the NLF as a separate delegation. Purely semantic concessions, but also some pressure from Washington, finally induced the Saigon government to go to Paris, but it was not until January 25, 1969, after President Nixon's inauguration, that the first session of the four parties dealing with the substance of the problem could be held.

From the terms for a settlement presented by each side at this session it was easy to see that prospects for an early peace were dim. Indeed, after three years and no fewer than 139 sessions of the four parties deliberating in Paris, and after almost two years of secret negotiations between Washington and Hanoi, the talks seemed to have reached a dead end at the beginning of 1972.

THE "VIETNAMIZATION" OF THE WAR

The financial burden of the war, rising popular opposition to it, and a growing conviction (shared now even by many former supporters of a win-the-war policy) that a favorable military decision was out of the question prompted the new President, Richard Nixon, to proclaim the ending of the Vietnam war as the major goal of his foreign policy. Three years later, however, the war was still going on, although U.S. participation in ground operations against the enemy had virtually ceased.

Two developments characterized the history of the Vietnamese war between 1969 and 1972. They are the massive withdrawal of American troops followed by a reduction of U.S. casualties from several hundred to less than ten per week, and the so-called Vietnamization of the war. As the United States withdrew more and more of its troops, the burden of the ground war was shifted to the South Vietnamese Army, whose weekly casualties consequently remained at their previous peak levels.

The U.S. troop withdrawals began with an announcement on June 8, 1969, that 25,000 men would leave Vietnam by the end of August. Two further withdrawals, of 35,000 and 50,000, were announced in September and December, 1969, respectively, and a plan to withdraw 150,000 more was revealed by President Nixon on April 20, 1970, leaving only 248,000 as of the spring of 1971, compared with 541,500 in March, 1969. During 1971, a total of 172,000 men were withdrawn, and on January 13, 1972, the President made another announcement that American troop strength would be reduced to 69,000 by May 1, 1972.

While these withdrawals gave the American people the impression that Mr. Nixon was seriously working toward "winding down" the war, the fighting not only continued but spread over the borders of Vietnam into Cambodia and also was intensified in Laos. Ten days after Mr. Nixon's announcement of April 20, 1970, that he would withdraw 150,000 more Americans, South Vietnamese and American troops invaded Cambodia, a widening of the war that proved, at least to the revived American opposition, that U.S. and South Vietnamese policy, in spite of all American troop withdrawals, still aimed at "winning" the war. American ground troops were withdrawn from Cambodia as of June 30, 1970, but U.S. air support for the South Vietnamese in Cambodia continued on a scale that devastated much of the country, killing tens of thousands of the people and creating at least 1.5 million refugees.

A steady increase of U.S. air activity over Vietnam, Cambodia, and Laos, next to building up, with American funds and equipment, the size and power of the South Vietnamese Army, was indeed the main feature of the so-called Vietnamization of the war. The aim of this policy was successfully to pursue the war with a well-equipped South Vietnamese Army of 1 million men even after all American combat troops had been withdrawn. As a result, the people of South Vietnam, Cambodia, and Laos suffered more from American bombing between 1969 and 1972, while American troops were being withdrawn under Nixon, than they had suffered under Johnson, when no fewer than half a million Americans were still engaged in or supporting the "search-and-destroy" operations against the enemy. Under Nixon, even the bombing of the North was resumed to some extent, under the slogan "protective reaction strikes," which culminated, in late 1971 and early 1972, in a series of raids as heavy as any conducted before the bombing halt on November 1, 1968. According to a report by the Cornell University Center for International Studies, the total tonnage of bombs dropped in the Nixon years from 1969 through 1971 was higher than that under Johnson from 1965 to 1968.

In February, 1971, the South Vietnamese Army, frustrated in Cambodia, attempted, with strong American air support, to invade Laos in order to cut the infiltration route from the North, the so-called Ho Chi Minh trail. This action revealed that Vietnamization was a possible policy for prolonging the war but a highly uncertain way of winning it. The invasion, a total failure, ended with a withdrawal, under North Vietnamese counterattacks, that "became a scramble for survival."[99] As of the spring of 1972, nothing had happened to demonstrate that the South Vietnamese and Americans could win a military victory in the South that would make it possible for them to impose their conditions for peace on the North.

Except for the increase of the monthly civilian toll from 95,000 in 1968 to 130,000 in 1971, nothing has changed for the people of Vietnam, Cambodia, and Laos since the withdrawal of most American troops from Indochina.

THE ENDLESS SEARCH FOR PEACE

Despite the policy of continuing the war through Vietnamization, extending it into Cambodia and Laos, the intensified air war all over Indochina, and the partial resumption of the bombing raids on the

North, there were, early in 1972, three elements that indicated the possibility of progress toward a peaceful settlement of the war. One was that Washington, although still conducting "protective reaction strikes," had abandoned the policy of trying to bomb Hanoi into accepting terms of surrender; another was the fact that, by accepting the Vietcong at the conference table, the United States had implicitly recognized the claim of the Communists for a role in determining the political future of South Vietnam; and finally, the withdrawal of American troops to a level of 69,000 by May 1, 1972, not only indicated a recognition that victory on the battlefield was impossible but also constituted a partial compliance with Hanoi's request that all U.S. and allied forces be withdrawn from Vietnam.

To this should be added that the Paris negotiations were not broken off by either side after three fruitless years but were actually supplemented during 1970 and 1971 by a series of secret talks between President Nixon's national security adviser, Dr. Henry A. Kissinger, and the chief spokesmen of the Hanoi and Vietcong delegations, as revealed by President Nixon on January 25, 1972. All this no doubt indicated a desire, at least on the part of Washington and Hanoi, to find a solution acceptable to both sides.

Nevertheless, a comparison of the latest Hanoi-Vietcong peace program with Mr. Nixon's eight-point proposal made public on January 25, 1972, demonstrated clearly that, after three years of talks, no basis for a political settlement had yet been found. To be sure, a major obstacle to such a settlement is the attitude of the South Vietnamese regime, which still hopes, through the U.S.-supported policy of Vietnamization, to force the enemy to become resigned and accept peace on Saigon's terms. But President Thieu may repeat his four "noes,"[100] which excluded any concession to the enemy, as often as he pleases; once Washington sees and accepts the fact that a political settlement requires a change of government in Saigon, Thieu's power to sabotage any compromise solution will have come to an end. The main obstacle to a political settlement, therefore, is the continued refusal by Washington to withdraw its support from the present Saigon regime.

Washington's refusal to take this decisive step is rooted in a fundamental misunderstanding of the trend of Vietnamese history and of Vietnam's contemporary political evolution. Since 1954, the United States has taken it upon itself to treat North and South Vietnam as two separate nations, disregarding the reality, historical and political, of a unified Vietnam in which political power, during the struggle against French colonial rule, tended to be concentrated in Communist hands. The Communists were about to establish effective control over all of Vietnam at the end of World War II without any outside assistance, and they would very likely have developed, independent of China, an Asian Titoist version of Communism, had not the French attempted to reconquer Indochina. The French attempt failed after nine years, under local political and military conditions that again favored a Communist regime for the whole of Vietnam. The settlement of the First Indochina War divided Vietnam at the Seventeenth Parallel into two military zones, a division that was to last only two years. To regard the people below and above this parallel as two separate nations was not only an absurd concept for anyone familiar with the history of Vietnam but also a legally untenable proposition, since the Geneva Agreement clearly envisaged the unification of the two zones through elections to be held in 1956, which every informed observer knew the Communists would win.

The Vietnamese conflict started in the late 1950's because the Communists were once more deprived of certain victory, this time by the United States, and because they were in danger of being exterminated by the Diem regime. It is a conflict essentially over the question of who shall control South Vietnam, and the related long-term question of whether and under whose auspices the reunification of the country will take place. After failing to sustain the regime in the South through diplomatic and financial assistance, the United States entered the war under the pretext that it had an obligation to come to the aid of an endangered ally, in total disregard of the fact that this ally was a mere creature of the United States and would not have existed if the Americans had not intervened in Indochina after the retreat of the French. With an attitude that has rightly been described as arrogance of power, the makers of American foreign policy acted under the assumption that American troops had more of a right to be in South Vietnam than had any Vietnamese soldier from the North and, furthermore, that the United States has as much right to play a role in determining the political future of Vietnam as have the Vietnamese themselves.

The manner in which this assumed American right is being exercised is poorly disguised behind assurances that the South Vietnamese people must have a chance to determine their political future. Such assurances have no meaning so long as Washington insists on procedures for this determination that in effect guarantee the present regime's continuance in power.

Seen in this light, which is the only way the Communists can possibly look at it, Nixon's eight-point proposal submitted to Hanoi and the Vietcong in secret talks in the fall of 1971 represents no progress at all over the terms for a settlement submitted at the beginning of the Paris negotiations. The crucial point of this program is Mr. Nixon's proposal that elections be held, supervised by a commission composed of all parties, and that President Thieu resign one month before these elections. With the American people, Mr. Nixon may have gained a temporary propaganda advantage with this proposal, but he did not advance the cause of peace in Vietnam. Anyone familiar with conditions in South Vietnam could have foreseen that the enemy would reject elections held with the powerfully entrenched administrative, military, and police apparatus of the present regime still intact, especially on the province and district level, where the henchmen of President Thieu exercise total control. Thieu's absence from the government would in no way alter the conditions under which these elections are to be held. With the effective help of this apparatus of power, which had already given him two election victories, Thieu or anyone of his kind could still run and would no doubt again "win" the election.

There will be no political settlement to end the war as long as the United States continues to maintain the present Saigon regime. It

I

is not true that the Communists insist on a government under their control as a condition for ending the war; all they demand is a coalition government composed of the NLF, the Saigon government without Thieu, and other existing groups not represented in the present government. They are willing to accept a mere share in power, no doubt because they are confident that, given freedom of expression and organization, they will sooner or later become the dominant force also in the South. If the Communists are right in their belief that, for them, full legality is a safe road to power, this solution will in all likelihood sooner or later also lead to a reunified Vietnam under Communist control.

For the people of Vietnam, this will not be the beginning of a better and freer way of life, something denied them for almost a century by the colonial regime and since 1954 by the postcolonial regimes in both the North and the South. But it will at last bring peace to a country that has suffered from war in one way or another since 1941.

To accept this outcome of the war after so many years of costly efforts to prevent it will be painful for many Americans and certainly also for many Vietnamese. But, for the people of Vietnam, history will not have come to an end. Their struggle for freedom and for a better life will be resumed, and will proceed under conditions infinitely more favorable than those existing as long as the war continues under the two rival dictatorships of the North and South. If this is not recognized by the United States and accepted as the only way to end the conflict, then no one can say how long the people of Indochina will continue to suffer and die in a war that should never have been fought.

POSTSCRIPT: JULY 12, 1972

Since the above outline of the prospects for a compromise settlement of the Vietnamese conflict was written, the war not only has been intensified by the offensive that the Communist side started on March 30 but also has once again been widened by President Nixon's decision to mine the harbors of North Vietnam, resume the bombing of the North on an unprecedented scale, and employ, to an extent never seen before, American air power in support of the South Vietnamese Army. The President's drastic military steps, no doubt considered necessary to stop the Communist offensive and prevent the collapse of the Thieu regime, were accompanied by continuing diplomatic efforts in Moscow and Peking and by a suspension, between May 4 and July 13, of the Paris peace talks. American troop withdrawals were to continue at a much slower rate in July and August than before, while the number of Americans employed in bombing Vietnam from Thailand and from a vastly enlarged American fleet off the Vietnamese coast almost doubled between April and mid-July, 1972. More bombs were dropped on Vietnam in the three months of April, May, and June, 1972, than fell on the country in a whole year during the bombing campaign under President Johnson. One hundred and fifty American aircraft were lost over North and South Vietnam between March 30 and July 1, increasing American casualties as well as the number of U.S. prisoners held by the enemy.

After some rather spectacular initial progress on several fronts, including the conquest of the city and the entire province of Quang Tri, the Communist offensive came to a half in early June. The exact reason for the halt cannot be determined until all the relevant military facts, as well as the political decisions of the parties involved in the conflict, are known. American military optimists like to believe that the offensive was stopped by the increased bombing of the enemy's positions and supply lines, together with effective resistance, after a few weeks of disarray, by the South Vietnamese Army. More skeptical observers attribute the halting of the offensive to deliberate military planning by the Communists or possibly to political considerations related to the expected reopening of the Paris talks. The Communists' shelling of South Vietnamese positions shows that the former still possess ample supplies, while the attempts of the South Vietnamese Army to regain some of the lost territory remain inconclusive.

Whether this turn of events, in particular the blockade of North Vietnam's harbors and the mild Chinese and Soviet reaction to it, will tempt Washington definitely to renounce its professed willingness to seek peace through political compromise and instead to pursue with new confidence the old policy of "winning" the war by bombing Hanoi into submission, only Nixon himself and perhaps a few of his closest advisers can tell at this time. If Washington and Saigon should continue to demand in the renewed peace talks what the enemy and most neutral observers rightly consider terms of surrender, and if Hanoi and the Vietcong should refuse to give up the struggle, it is impossible to foresee what would happen. But it is likely that the war would continue, with unlimited American bombing in both North and South, even though the blockade might significantly reduce the enemy's supplies and force him to return to small-scale guerrilla operations. As the past fifteen years have shown, guerrilla warfare can be maintained over a long period.

The new bombing, however, although nearly genocidal in character, may again fail to achieve its military and political objectives. Nixon knows that the American people expect him to get out of the war by the November, 1972, elections and that the voters may not accept his policy of seeking peace by extending the war and of trying to bring American prisoners home by increasing their numbers. Moreover, Moscow and Peking are not likely to let the President have his "honorable" peace until or unless he makes some of the political concessions demanded by Hanoi and the National Liberation Front. Nevertheless, not only Peking and Moscow but Hanoi, too, may wisely allow Washington to camouflage any American concessions with the claim that the energetic policy Nixon adopted in April and his negotiations with China and the Soviet Union have forced the enemy to retreat. The enemy may have started his offensive only to improve his military position in anticipation of a cease-fire, the main American condition for a complete withdrawal from Vietnam. But unless Washington makes some political concessions, necessarily at the expense of Saigon, there will be no cease-fire. Even minor concessions may be acceptable to Hanoi and the Vietcong in exchange for a cease-fire. The Communists, whose strength has always been political rather than military, may settle for a small share of power for some time, thus enabling Nixon to say that he has prvented the imposition of a Communist regime in South Vietnam. A resolution of the conflict on this basis may offer the United States the only honorable way to get out of the war and, for the Communists in the South, may very likely mean only a delay on their road to power.

Notes

CHAPTER 2.
PREHISTORY AND CHINESE RULE

1. This theory originated with the French historian E. Chavannes and was supported by Leonard Aurousseau. For Chavannes, see his *Mémoires historiques de Se-ma T'sien*, 6 vols. (Paris, 1895–1905). Aurousseau developed the same theory in his article "Notes sur les origines du peuple annamite," in *Bulletin de l'École Française d'Extrême Orient* 23 (1923): 263.

2. The first scholar who attacked the theory that no proto-Vietnamese population existed in the Red River delta before the arrival of one branch of the Viet was Henri Maspéro, in an essay on the origin of the Vietnamese people in *T'oung pao*, of December, 1924. See also Le Thanh Khoi, *Le Viet-Nam: Histoire et civilisation* (Paris, 1955), pp. 88 ff.

3. The most up-to-date study of the prehistoric migrations and racial fusions in the Indochinese peninsula is contained in Georges Coedès, *The Making of Southeast Asia* (Berkeley, Calif., 1964).

4. For a closer study of the Dong Son culture, see Victor Goloubew, "L'age du bronze au Tonkin et dans le Nord-Annam" in *Bulletin de l'École Française d'Extrême Orient* 29 (1929): 1–46, and *idem*, *L'archéologie du Tonkin et les fouilles du Dong-Son* (Hanoi, 1937). Also H. Mansuy, *La Préhistoire en Indochine* (Paris, 1931).

5. The theory that the races inhabiting Indochina as well as all of Southeast
   Asia came from southern China and Tibet was first formulated by two
   Austrian anthropologists, Father F. W. Schmidt and R. von Heine-Geldern.
   Cf. also the leading authority on the history of Southeast Asia, D. G. E.
   Hall, *A History of South East Asia* (New York, 1955; London, 1966).

6. For more about the relationship between the Vietnamese language and Mon-
   Khmer, as well as the various Thai dialects, see the articles by Henri Maspéro
   and J. Przyluski in Meillet and Cohen, *Les langues du monde*, 2d ed. (Paris,
   1953), as well as Charles Robequain, *L'Indochine*, 3d ed. (Paris, 1952).

7. See Huard and Bigot, *Les caractéristiques anthropo-biologiques des Indochinois*
   (Hanoi, 1938); also Pierre Huard and Maurice Durand, *Connaissance du
   Viet-Nam* (Paris and Hanoi, 1954), particularly Chapters III and IV.

8. See Le Thanh Khoi, *op. cit.* (n. 2, above), who gives a description of pre-
   Chinese Vietnamese society (p. 87) based largely on Henri Maspéro, "Le
   royaume de Van Laung," in *Bulletin de l'École Française d'Extrême Orient*,
   Vol. 37 (1937).

9. For a more detailed description with further reference to sources, see Joseph
   Buttinger, *The Smaller Dragon* (New York, 1958), pp. 111–12.

10. For Van Lang, see Maspéro, *op. cit.* (n. 8, above), and Huard and Durand,
    op. cit. (n. 7, above), p. 8; for Au Lac, Huard and Durand, *ibid.*, pp.
    10–11.

11. According to some of my Vietnamese scholar-friends, recent anthropological
    finds in North Vietnam give conclusive evidence of a much older pre-Chinese
    culture in the Red River delta than hitherto assumed; these finds also seem to
    confirm the existence of a Vietnamese state, probably Van Lang, many
    centuries before the Chinese conquest.

12. For more on Nam Viet, see Le Thanh Khoi, *op. cit.* (n. 2), pp. 91–97.

13. For a detailed description of the spread of Indian cultural influence in
    Indochina, see Hall, *op. cit.* (n. 5, above), Chapter 2, pp. 12–22, and John F.
    Cady, *Southeast Asia; Its Historical Development* (New York, 1964), Chapter
    2, "Trade Patterns and the Process of Indianization," pp. 21–48. The main
    works on Funan and Champa are Georges Coedès, *The Indianized States of
    Southeast Asia* (Honolulu, 1964), and Georges Maspéro, *Le royaume de
    Champa* (Paris, 1928). A translation of Chapter I of Maspéro's work has
    appeared in English under the title *The Kingdom of Champa* (New Haven,
    Conn., 1949). See also Hall, pp. 23–28; Cady, Part Two, Chapter 3; and
    Coedès, *Making of Southeast Asia* (n. 3, above), Part Two, Chapter 2 and 3,
    pp. 50–68.

14. On Cham art, see H. Parmentier, *Les sculptures Chames au musée de Tourane*
    (Paris, 1922), and Jeanne Leuba, *Un royaume disparu: Les Chams et leur art*
    (Paris, 1923).

15. Buttinger, *op. cit.* (n. 9, above), p. 96.

16. A listing of ten major Vietnamese uprisings against Chinese rule is contained
    in *ibid.*, pp. 177–78.

17. On the conquest of Vietnam by China and the 1,000 years of Chinese rule,

see also Le Thanh Khoi, *op. cit.* (n. 2, above), Chapter II, pp. 98–134, and Georges Coedès, *Making of Southeast Asia*, Part Two, Chapter i, pp. 39–49.

CHAPTER 3.
INDEPENDENCE AND EXPANSION

18. The chief sources about the victorious revolution led by Ngo Quyen are the *Imperial Annals of Annam*, translated from the Chinese by Abel des Michels and published in Paris in two volumes in 1892.

19. This was Co Loa, said to have been the capital of Au Lac, upstream from Hanoi. The city of Hanoi was founded by the Chinese. Of Co Loa, three ramparts are still preserved. See Gustave Dumoutier, *Étude historique et archéologique sur Co-loa* (Paris, 1893).

20. Under the Ly and the Tran, the name of the capital was changed to Thang Long. Its old Chinese name, Dong Kinh, i.e., "Capital of the East," was restored in 1428. This name was later erroneously applied by Westerners to the entire North of Vietnam, which they called Tongking or Tonkin.

21. The Ly rulers were ardent Buddhists. Under their reign, Buddhist pagodas acquired large domains through royal grants.

22. Ho Qui Ly had already decreed his radical land reform as regent of the Tran ruler in 1397. Except for princes and princesses of royal blood, no one was allowed more than 10 mau (about 8.8 acres) of land.

23. For detailed descriptions of the conquest of Champa and the decline of Cambodia, see Charles Maybon, *Histoire moderne du pays d'Annam* (Paris, 1920), and L. P. Briggs, *The Ancient Khmer Empire* (Philadelphia, 1951). Also Georges Maspéro, *L'empire Khmer* (Paris, 1914). For a brief explanation of the decline of the Cambodian empire, see Hall, *op. cit.* (n. 5, above), p. 111.

24. Alexander of Rhodes's important books are: *Relations des heureux succès de la foi au royaume de Tonkin* (Paris, 1650); *Histoire du Tonkin* (Paris, 1652); and *Divers voyages et missions* (Paris, 1953). An English version of this last book appeared under the title *Rhodes of Viet Nam* (Westminster, 1966).

25. The literature in English on this long period of Vietnamese history, from the beginning of independence to the reign of Gia Long, is unfortunately not profuse. The reader who desires a more detailed knowledge of post-Chinese and precolonial Vietnam still has to rely on the main works in French, primarily Le Thanh Khoi, *op. cit.* (n. 2, above), Chapters III through VII. The work of another author, Jean Chesneaux, a Marxist scholar like Le Thanh Khoi, has become available in English under the title *The Vietnamese Nation* (Sydney, Australia, 1966). It is a translation of *Contributions à l'histoire de la nation Vietnamienne* (Paris, 1955), and is especially important for an understanding of the economic and social conditions of precolonial Vietnam. For this same

period, the English reader is advised also to study Hall, *op. cit.* (n. 5), Part 1, Chapter 2; Part II, Chapter 22; and Part III, Chapter 34. For a brief survey of Vietnamese history from its origins to the present, see also Chester A. Bain, *Vietnam: The Roots of Conflict* (Englewood Cliffs, N.J., 1967). Also available in English, giving the point of view of the Vietnamese nationalist historians, is Nguyen Van Thai and Nguyen Van Mung, *A Short History of Vietnam* (Saigon, 1958). In Buttinger, *op. cit.* (n. 9), the period is covered in Chapters III, IV, and V.

26. For a searching and still unsurpassed study of the evolution of French policy in Asia up to and through the period of the conquest of Indochina, see John F. Cady, *The Roots of French Imperialism in Eastern Asia* (Ithaca, N.Y., 1954). Another essential work on this period, covering also French policy toward Vietnam in the seventeenth and eighteenth centuries, is Georges Taboulet, *La geste française en Indochine*, 2 vols. (Paris, 1955, 1956).

CHAPTER 4.
THE CENTURY OF COLONIALISM

27. For this period of the conquest, see Taboulet, *op. cit.* (n. 26, above), 2: 429–56.
28. See Cady, *op. cit.* (n. 13, above), pp. 267 ff. Also Hall, *op. cit.* (n. 5), pp. 560–65.
29. See Francis Garnier's main work, *Voyage d'exploration de l'Indochine*, 2 vols. (Paris, 1885).
30. These events are described in a series of documents in Taboulet, *op. cit.* (n. 26, above) 2, Book VI: 674–738.
31. On the entire period of armed resistance to French rule from the uprising in Cochinchina in 1863 to the end of the resistance in Tongking in 1897, see Nguyen Van Thai and Nguyen Van Mung, *op. cit.* (n. 25, above), Chapter X, pp. 300–15. Also Joseph Buttinger, *Vietnam: A Dragon Embattled*, 2 vols. (New York, 1967; London, 1967), especially Vol. I, Chapter III, "The Movements of National Resistance."
32. On Paul Doumer and his role in the making of French Indochina, see above all his own book, *L'Indo-Chine française: Souvenirs* (Paris, 1903). Also important are Paul Isoart, *Le phénomène national vietnamien: De l'indépendance unitaire à l'indépendance fractionée* (Paris, 1961); and on the economics of colonialism, Charles Robequain, *The Economic Development of French Indo-China* (London, 1944). The main work in English on the entire period of colonial rule up to 1936 is Virginia Thompson, *French Indochina* (London, 1937). Other works in English are Stephen H. Roberts, *History of French Colonial Policy: 1870–1925*, 2 vols. (London, 1929), and Thomas E. Ennis, *French Policy and Developments in Indochina* (Chicago, 1956). For a critique of Doumer's policies, and the economic policies of the French in

Indochina generally, see Fernand Bernard, *L'Indo-Chine, erreurs et dangers: Un programme* (Paris, 1901), and Paul Bernard, *Le Problème économique indochinois* (Paris, 1934). A modern treatment of the French in Indochina, covering conquest and colonial rule, the reader will find in John F. Cady, *Southeast Asia: Its Historical Development* (New York, 1964), Part Five, Chapter 18, pp. 406–34.

33. See Lauriston Sharp, "Colonial Regimes in Southeast Asia," in *Far Eastern Survey*, Feb. 27, 1946, for further details. The antisocial policies of the colonial regime were most severely attacked by visiting French journalists, who, as a rule, were shocked by the conditions of the indigenous population. Among these authors are Jean Ajalbert, *L'Indochine en peril* (Paris, 1906), and *idem, Les nuages sur L'Indochine* (Paris, 1912); Roland Dorgèles, *Sur la route mandarine* (Paris, 1929); and Georges Garros, *Forceries humaines* (Paris, 1926). See also Ho Chi Minh, *Selected Works*, 3 vols. (Hanoi, 1960 and 1961).

34. On the failure of the old resistance movements, see Le Thanh Khoi, *op. cit.* (n. 2, above) pp. 384–85, and Buttinger, *Vietnam: Dragon Embattled* (n. 31) 1: 138–44.

35. On the Vietnamese student in Japan, see Ennis, *op. cit.* (n. 32, above), pp. 178 ff.

36. A vast and growing literature on Phan Boi Chau exists, but unfortunately mostly in Vietnamese. For a partial listing, see Buttinger, *Vietnam: Dragon Embattled* (n. 31, above) 1: 512–13, note 69. For Chau's own writing, *ibid.*, 1: 517, note 78.

37. See Louis Roubaud, *Viet-Nam: La tragédie indochinoise* (Paris, 1931), and Andrée Viollis', *Indochine S.O.S.* (Paris, 1935). On these, but still more on subsequent events, the reader will profit from a study of two works in English, Ellen Hammer's pioneering *The Struggle for Indochina* (Stanford, Calif., 1954), and Donald Lancaster, *The Emancipation of French Indochina* (London, 1961). The most complete study of the parties and groups in the entire nationalist movement is Pierre Dabezies, *Forces politiques au Viet-Nam*, which unfortunately exists only in mimeographed copies in a few libraries. No date (1957?).

38. See Milton Sacks's study "Marxism in Vietnam," in Frank Trager, ed., *Marxism in Southeast Asia: A Study of Four Countries* (Stanford, Calif., 1959). On the life and political role of Ho Chi Minh, see Robert Shaplen, "The Enigma of Ho Chi Minh," *The Reporter*, January 27, 1955, and Jean Lacouture, *Ho Chi Minh* (New York and London, 1968), the most up-to-date and comprehensive biography of the outstanding leader of Vietnamese Communism.

39. See Viollis, *op. cit.*, and Hammer, *op. cit.* (both n. 37, above), pp. 84–86. Also Le Thanh Khoi, *op. cit.* (n. 2), Chapter IX, pp. 435 ff.

40. On these sects, see Bernard B. Fall, "The Political-Religious Sects of Vietnam," *Pacific Affairs*, Vol. 28 (September, 1955). Also Lancaster, *op. cit.*, (n. 37, above), pp. 86, 88, and 381.

41. On the Japanese occupation of Vietnam, see Lancaster, *op. cit.*, Part II, Chapter VI; Hammer, *op. cit.*, (both n. 37, above) Chapters One and Two; and Buttinger, *Vietnam: Dragon Embattled* (n. 31), Vol. 1, Chapter V.

42. For a defense of French cooperation with the Japanese, see Jean Decoux, *A la barre de l'Indochine: Histoire de mon gouvernement général, 1940–1945* (Paris, 1952). This period is also covered by one of the most important books on the modern history of Vietnam, Philippe Devillers, *Histoire du Viet-Nam, de 1940 à 1952* (Paris, 1952).

43. On this important phase in the activities of Ho Chi Minh and his nationalist opponents in China, King C. Chen, *Vietnam and China, 1938–1954* (Princeton, N.J., 1969), throws entirely new light, since the author was the first to gain access to Chinese Nationalist archives on Taiwan. Much of what has been written before on the activities of the Vietnamese exiles in China prior to 1945 will have to be revised in the light of Chen's new information.

44. See Devillers, *op. cit.* (n. 42, above), especially pp. 132–44. Also Hammer, *op. cit.*, Chapter Four, p. 98, and Lancaster, *op. cit.* (both n. 37), Part III, Chapter VII, pp. 111–22.

CHAPTER 5.
INDEPENDENCE AND WAR

45. These events are most vividly described by Devillers, *op. cit.* (n. 42, above), pp. 132–43. See also Hammer *op. cit.*, Chapter Four, pp. 98–105, and Lancaster, *op. cit.* (both n. 37), pp. 111–20.

46. See the description and analysis of the so-called March Declaration of the French Government in Buttinger, *Vietnam: Dragon Embattled* (n. 31, above) 1: 609–10, note 3 to Chapter VI. Bernard B. Fall, in his *The Two Viet-Nams*, 2d rev. ed., (London, 1963; New York, 1967), has this to say on the March Declaration: "That program, which might have been considered a step forward in 1925 or 1935, no longer had any correspondence with the situation inside Indochina" (p. 66).

47. See Jean Sainteny, *Histoire d'une paix manquée* (Paris, 1953), one of the most important inside accounts of French policy toward Indochina during 1945 and 1946.

48. See Hammer, *op. cit.* (n. 37, above), pp. 110–19.

49. An American correspondent, Harold Isaacs, has given a firsthand account of Anglo-French cooperation in the suppression of the nationalist revolution in the South in his book *No Peace for Asia* (New York, 1947). Isaacs also showed that Japanese troops were employed by the British and French against the Vietnamese (pp. 158–59). See also Devillers, *op. cit.* (n. 42, above), pp. 163–76.

50. See Devillers, *op. cit.* (n. 42, above), p. 167.

51. About the behavior of the Chinese occupation troops in North Vietnam, see the report of another American correspondent, Robert Trumbull, *The Scru-*

table East (New York, 1964), especially p. 201. See also Isaacs, *op. cit.* (n. 49, above), pp. 168–69; Sainteny, *op. cit.* (n. 47), p. 150, and the extensive report on the Chinese occupation by another Frenchman, Pierre Celerier (pseud.) in *Menaces sur le Viet-Nam* (Saigon, 1950).

52. On these Viet Minh maneuvers, and especially the elections, see Hammer, *op. cit.* (n. 37, above), pp. 142–44; Devillers, *op. cit.* (n. 42), pp. 200–201; and Le Thanh Khoi, who gives the exact figures of deputies obtained by the various parties, *op. cit.* (n. 2), p. 468. See also Sainteny, *op. cit.* (n. 47), p. 171.

53. For the full English text of the Sino-French treaty of February 28, 1946, see Harold Isaacs, *New Cycle in Asia* (New York, 1947), pp. 166–68.

54. The most interesting description of the negotiations that led to the March agreement is given by Sainteny, *op. cit.* (n. 47, above). For the text of the March agreement, see Isaacs, *New Cycle in Asia* (n. 53), p. 169. On the March agreement, see further Allan B. Cole, ed., *Conflict in Indochina and International Repercussions: A Documentary History, 1945–1955* (Ithaca, N.Y., 1956), pp. 40–42, and Hammer, *op. cit.* (n. 37), p. 157.

55. For details on the retreat of the leaders of the anti–Viet Minh nationalists into Chinese exile, see Devillers, *op. cit.* (n. 42, above), p. 279; Isoart, *op. cit.* (n. 32), p. 365; and Hammer, *op. cit.* (n. 37), p. 176. Devillers's is also the most informative account of the anti–Viet Minh activities of the VNQDD and Dong Minh Hoi and of their final elimination.

56. D'Argenlieu said he was "amazed" that, despite the fact that France had such a fine expeditionary corps in Indochina, "its leaders prefer to negotiate rather than to fight." Hammer, *op. cit.* (n. 37, above), p. 155.

57. See *ibid.*, p. 158. On the maneuvers of d'Argenlieu to undermine the March agreement, see also Lancaster, *op. cit.* (n. 37, above), pp. 139 and 152.

58. See the comments on d'Argenlieu's maneuvers by the two outstanding French journalist-historians, Philippe Devillers and Jean Lacouture, in the English edition of their book *La fin d'une guerre: Indochine 1954* (1960), which appeared under the title *End of a War: Indochina, 1954* (London, 1968; New York, 1969), especially pp. 9–11.

59. The most informative account of the Dalat and Fontainebleau conferences, as well as of the reasons for their failure, is still Devillers, *Histoire du Viet-Nam* (n. 42, above), pp. 256 ff. and pp. 289 ff. See also Lancaster, *op. cit.*, p. 162, and Hammer, *op. cit.* (both n. 37), pp. 166–67. For the text of the *modus vivendi*, see Cole, ed., *op. cit.* (n. 54, above), p. 46. An important work on French policy in Vietnam, covering also the phase prior to the outbreak of the Indochina War, is Paul Mus, *Viet-Nam: Sociologie d'une guerre* (Paris, 1950), parts of which have been translated into English by John T. McAlister and published under the title *The Vietnamese and Their Revolution* (London, 1969; New York, 1970). McAlister made an important contribution for an understanding of the events in Vietnam in his *Viet Nam: The Origins of Revolution* (New York, 1969).

60. On the Haiphong incident, see Hammer, *op. cit.*, p. 183; Lancaster, *op. cit.*

(both n. 37, above), pp. 170–71; and Paul Mus in *Témoignage Chrétien*, August 12, 1949. Vietnamese estimates were that, on this day, at least 20,000 Vietnamese were killed. A strictly Viet Minh account of the Haiphong incident is to be found in an article by Henri Larroue, "Comment a débuté la guerre du Viet-Nam," in *Cahiers internationaux*, No. 40, November, 1952.

61. A description of these events is contained in Philippe Devillers, "Vietnamese Nationalism and French Politics," in William L. Holland, ed., *Asian Nationalism and the West* (New York, 1953).

62. On these military events, see Edgar O'Ballance, *The Indochina War 1945–1954: A Study in Guerrilla Warfare* (London, 1964). Also Bernard Fall, *Street Without Joy: Insurgency in Indochina* (Harrisburg, Pa., 1961; London, 1963): There exist a great number of books on the First Indochina War, mostly in French, of which very few are available in English. One of these is the rather sensational book by Lucien Bodard, *The Quicksand War* (Boston and London, 1967), describing, in addition to the cruelties of the war, also the corruption in Saigon, French as well as Vietnamese.

63. On the failure of the Bao Dai solution, see Devillers in Holland, ed., *op. cit.* (n. 61, above); Hammer, *op. cit.*, Chapter Eleven; and Lancaster, *op. cit.* (both n. 37), Chapter XI.

64. The list of books on the battle of Dien Bien Phu is long. For the English reader, the two most important books are Bernard B. Fall, *Hell in a Very Small Place: The Siege of Dien Bien Phu* (London, 1965; Philadelphia and New York, 1967); and Jules Roy, *The Battle of Dien Bien Phu* (New York and London, 1965). See also Henri Navarre, *Agonie de l'Indochine* (Paris, 1956), for the view of the French military, and Vo Nguyen Giap, *Dien Bien Phu* (Hanoi, 1954), for the assessment of the famous battle by the commander of the Viet Minh forces.

65. The three most important books on the Geneva Conference are Robert F. Randle, *Geneva, 1954: The Settlement of the Indochina War* (Princeton, N.J., 1969); Devillers and Lacouture, *End of a War* (n. 58, above); and Victor Bator, *Viet-Nam: A Diplomatic Tragedy* (Dobbs Ferry, N.Y., 1965; London, 1967). See also Sir Anthony Eden, *Full Circle: Memoirs of Sir Anthony Eden* (Boston, 1960); Melvin Gurtov, *The First Vietnam Crisis* (London and New York, 1968); and, for documents and texts relating to the Geneva Conference, Marvin E. Gettleman, *Vietnam: History, Documents and Opinions on a Major World Crisis* (New York, 1965). For a critical assessment by an American participant in the conference, see Chester L. Cooper, *The Lost Crusade: America in Vietnam* (New York, 1970; London, 1971), Chapter IV.

66. For a critical survey of the achievements and failures of the Hanoi regime, see P. J. Honey, ed., *North Vietnam Today: Profile of a Communist Satellite* (New York, 1962). For a more balanced view, see Fall, *The Viet-Nams* (n. 46, above).

67. Much has been written about the role allegedly played by official and non-

official Americans in the appointment of Ngo Dinh Diem in June, 1954. The most up-to-date and most accurate version of this frequently distorted story is told by Cooper, *op. cit.* (n. 65, above), Chapter VI, "Birth of a Non-Nation," pp. 115–43.

68. Since about 1968, books on Vietnam in English, written chiefly by Americans, have begun to outnumber French books on Vietnam, and on the whole they also surpass them in the quality of their information and judgment. This is true especially for books on the Diem regime. The typical French view on this period is presented by Georges Chaffard in his *Indochine: Dix ans d'indépendence* (Paris, 1964). The best American book on the Diem regime is Robert Scigliani, *South Vietnam: Nation Under Stress* (Boston, 1963). See also David Halberstam, *The Making of a Quagmire* (London and New York, 1965); John Mecklin, *Mission in Torment: An Intimate Account of the U.S. Role in Vietnam* (Garden City, N.Y., 1965); Denis Warner, *The Last Confucian* (New York, 1963; London, 1964); Fall, *Two Viet-Nams* (n. 46, above); and for a broader view, putting the Diem regime into the context of recent Vietnamese history, Robert Shaplen, *The Lost Revolution: The U.S. in Vietnam, 1946–1966*, rev. ed. (New York, 1966). Wesley R. Fishel, ed., *Problems of Freedom: South Vietnam Since Independence* (Chicago, 1961), is largely a defense of the Diem regime by twelve authors, some of whom had already changed their minds when the book appeared. For the critical views of a former official of the Diem regime, see Nguyen Thai, *Is South Viet-Nam Viable?* (Manila, 1962).

69. The best account of the events that culminated in the fall of Diem is in Shaplen, *op. cit.* (n. 68, above), pp. 188–212. See also Halberstam, *op. cit.* (n. 68), Chapter XVII, pp. 277–99.

CHAPTER 6.
THE SECOND INDOCHINA WAR

70. For a survey, highly critical, of the gradual U.S. involvement in Vietnam and the beginning of the Second Indochina War, see George McTurnan Kahin and John W. Lewis, *The United States in Vietnam* (New York, 1967). See also Cooper, *op. cit.* (n. 65, above), Chapters VII through XII.

71. Already in March, 1965, Assistant Secretary of Defense John McNaughton had defined the U.S. aims in Vietnam quite frankly as follows: 70 per cent to avoid humiliating defeat, 20 per cent to keep Vietnam out of Chinese hands, and 10 per cent to permit the people of South Vietnam to enjoy, a better, freer way of life. *Pentagon Papers* (New York: Bantam Books, 1971), Document No. 96, pp. 432–40.

72. *Ibid.*, p. 523.

73. *Ibid.*, p. 67.

74. *Ibid.*, p. 75.

75. *Ibid.*, p. 77.

76. See the statement made by General Earl G. Wheeler on the threatened collapse of the South Vietnamese armed forces, as quoted by Theodore Draper in his *Abuse of Power* (New York, 1967; London, 1969), p. 84.

77. See *The New York Times* of November 13, 1966.

78. For more details about corruption in South Vietnam, see David Halberstam's report in *Harper's Magazine*, December, 1967.

79. See Robert Shaplen, "Letter from Vietnam," *The New Yorker*, November 13, 1971.

80. *Pentagon Papers*, Document No. 120, pp. 553–55.

81. *Ibid.*, Document No. 132, pp. 615–21.

82. Robert Shaplen in *The New Yorker*, March 23, 1968.

83. Charles Mohr in *The New York Times*, March 20, 1968. See also Robert Shaplen in *The New Yorker*, March 23, 1968, who said that by early March the Vietcong had recruited at least 30,000 fresh troops.

84. *Pentagon Papers*, p. 601.

85. U.S. Senate, Subcommittee on Refugees, hearings on April 21 and 22, 1971.

86. Indochina Resources Center, Washington, D.C.

87. For a graphic account of the destruction of a large village and the removal and resettlement of the population, see Jonathan Schell, *The Village of Ben Suc* (New York, 1967).

88. Edward Kennedy, "'The Other War' in Vietnam," *The New Leader*, November 20, 1967.

89. *Ibid.*

90. On destruction and casualties in the North see Harrison Salisbury, *Behind the Lines—Hanoi* (New York, 1967), especially Chapter X.

91. *Pentagon Papers*, Document No. 101, pp. 491–93.

92. *Ibid.*, Document No. 120, pp. 553–55.

93. Senator Vance Hartke in the *Saturday Evening Post*, April 22, 1967.

94. *Pentagon Papers*, Document No. 129, pp. 577–85.

95. For evidence that Washington expected Hanoi to reject the President's proposal to negotiate, see *Pentagon Papers*, Document No. 134, pp. 622–23.

96. *Ibid.*, p. 388.

97. *Ibid.*, Document No. 103, pp. 449–54. Emphasis in the original.

98. On previous American "peace proposals" and why they failed, see David Kraslow and Stuart Loory, *The Secret Search for Peace* (New York, 1968); also Eugene McCarthy, "Pentagon Papers," *The New Republic*, July 10, 1971.

99. *Time* Magazine, January 3, 1972.

100. The four "noes" are: no territorial concessions to the Communists, no free political activity for the Communists, no coalition government, and no "neutralism."

Selected Bibliography

Since the end of the Indochina War in 1954, there has been in the Western world an outpouring of books on Vietnam and former French Indochina that can only be described as inflationary. One aspect of the phenomenon is the vast increase in English titles, which quickly overtook the previously dominating output in French. In fact, of the many hundred volumes on Vietnam that have appeared since the early 1960's, eight out of ten were written in English.

This change can be illustrated by the proportion of French and English titles in the bibliographies of the books I have published on Vietnam. Of the nearly 600 titles in the bibliography of *The Smaller Dragon* (published in 1958), 490 are in French and fewer than 100 in English. Of the 312 titles in *Vietnam: A Dragon Embattled*, which brings the history up to the end of 1963, 188 are in English, while the French run only to 124. This tendency becomes even more pronounced in the bibliography of *Vietnam: A Political History* (published in 1968), of which the titles in French are reduced to 33 compared to 127 in English.

In keeping with the size and purpose of this new book, the bibliographical list has been kept considerably shorter (57 titles). These do not include all the books and other sources listed in the notes to the four center chapters on the history of Vietnam. Since these chapters deal largely with events prior to 1954, it is not surprising that 42 of the 92 titles are still in French. However, the list of 57

J

books that follows contains no more than 13 French authors in their original
language, compared to 44 in English.

AJALBERT, JEAN. *Les nuages sur l'Indochine*. Paris: Louis Michaud, 1912. A visiting
    French journalist's slashing critique of the social and political conditions
    created by the colonial regime in Vietnam.
AUSTIN, ANTHONY. *The President's War: The Story of the Tonkin Gulf Resolution
    and How the Nation Was Trapped in Vietnam*. A New York Times Book. New
    York and Philadelphia: J. B. Lippincott Company, 1971.
BAIN, CHESTER A. *Vietnam: The Roots of Conflict*. Englewood Cliffs, N.J.:
    Prentice-Hall, 1967. A brief history of Vietnam from the origin of the
    country to the beginning of U.S. military intervention.
BATOR, VICTOR. *Viet-Nam: A Diplomatic Tragedy*. Dobbs Ferry, N.Y.: Oceana
    Publications, 1965. A critic of Washington's diplomatic strategy prior to and
    during the Geneva Conference of 1954.
BERNARD, PAUL. *Le problème économique indochinois*. Paris: Nouvelles Editions
    Latines, 1934. A critique by a French expert of the colonial regime's anti-
    developmental economic policies.
BROWNE, MALCOLM W. *The New Face of War*. Rev. ed. London: Cassell,
    1958; Indianapolis, Ind., and New York: The Bobbs-Merrill Company,
    1968. Describes the failure of Diem's army to cope with the fighting tech-
    niques of the Vietcong and the political decline of the Diem regime.
BURCHETT, WILFRED G. *The Furtive War: The United States in Vietnam and
    Laos*. New York: International Publishers, 1963. The Communist view of
    the war, as seen by a veteran Australian journalist.
————.*Vietnam: Inside Story of the Guerrilla War*. New York: International
    Publishers, 1965. A follow-up on *The Furtive War* based on firsthand obser-
    vation in Vietcong areas.
BUTTINGER, JOSEPH. *Vietnam: A Political History*. New York: Praeger Publishers,
    1968; London: Deutsch, 1969. A condensed edition of the author's three-
    volume history, *The Smaller Dragon* and *Vietnam: A Dragon Embattled*, with
    a new chapter on the Americanization of the Vietnamese war.
CADY, JOHN F. *Southeast Asia: Its Historical Development*. New York: McGraw-
    Hill Book Company, 1964. A scholarly and up-to-date history of the entire
    region with extensive chapters on Vietnam.
CHAPPOULIÉ, HENRI. *Aux origines d'une église: Rome et les missions d'Indochine
    au XVIIe siècle*. 2 vols. Paris: Bloud and Gay, 1943–47. The main work on
    the Catholic missions in Vietnam.
CHESNEAUX, JEAN, *The Vietnamese Nation*. Sydney, Australia: Current Books,

1966. Studies by a French Marxist covering aspects of ancient and colonial history of Vietnam. Translated from the French. (*Contributions à l'histoire de la nation vietnamienne*, Paris, 1955.)

COOPER, CHESTER L. *The Lost Crusade*. New York: Dodd, Mead and Company, 1970; London: MacGibbon & Kee, 1971. An all-embracing survey of the United States involvement by a high Administration official (Assistant for Asian Affairs on the White House Staff and U.S. delegate at the Geneva Conference, 1954, and the 1961–62 Conference on Laos). Cooper worked tirelessly to promote a peaceful settlement of the Vietnam war.

DEVILLERS, PHILIPPE. *Histoire du Viet-Nam de 1940 à 1952*. Paris: Editions du Seuil, 1952. A French journalist-historian's outstanding account of French policy in Vietnam during and after World War II. Indispensable for an understanding of Communist strength in Vietnam and the failure of the French in fighting the Viet Minh.

DEVILLERS, PHILIPPE, and JEAN LACOUTURE, *End of a War: Indochina, 1954*. New York: Praeger Publishers, 1969. A book published in France in 1960, describing the collapse of the French military effort in Indochina. Enlightening also about the proceedings at the Geneva Conference of 1954.

DUMAREST, ANDRÉ. *La formation des classes sociales en pays annimite*. Lyons: Imprimerie Ferréol, 1935. An analysis of the social structure of colonial Vietnam.

FALL, BERNARD B. *Hell in a Very Small Place: The Siege of Dien Bien Phu*. London: Pall Mall, 1965; Philadelphia and New York: J. B. Lippincott Company, 1967. The dramatic story of the battle that led to the end of the Indochina War 1946–54.

————. *The Two Viet-Nams: A Political and Military Analysis*. London: Pall Mall, 1963; 2nd. rev. ed. New York: Praeger Publishers, 1967. A critical account of both North and South Vietnam.

————.*Viet-Nam Witness, 1953–66*. New York: Praeger Publishers, 1966. A collection of articles by the well-known authority on Vietnam who was killed while accompanying an American patrol in February, 1967.

FISHEL, WESLEY R., ed. *Problems of Freedom: South Vietnam Since Independence*. Chicago: Free Press of Glencoe, 1961. Contains papers presented at a conference in New York in October, 1959, organized by the American Friends of Vietnam. The contributors: Joseph Buttinger, John C. Donnell, John T. Dorsey, Jr., Wesley R. Fishel, William Henderson, James B. Hendry, Wolf Ladejinsky, Craig S. Lichtenwalner, Robert R. Nathan, Edgar N. Pike, Tran Ngoc Lien, and Vu Van Thai. With an introduction by Senator Mike Mansfield.

GETTLEMAN, MARVIN E. *Vietnam: History, Documents and Opinions on a Major World Crisis*. New York: Fawcett World Library, 1965. Documents, excerpts from books, articles, official statements, etc., with introductory comments by Mr. Gettleman, ranging from precolonial Vietnam to 1965.

GOSSELIN, CHARLES. *L'empire d'Annam*. Paris: Perrin, 1904. A history of precolonial Vietnam and of the conquest of Indochina by France written by an officer who took part in the conquest.

GURTOV, MELVIN. *The First Vietnam Crisis*. New York: Columbia University Press, 1967. A perceptive analysis of Chinese Communist strategy and U.S. involvement in the events of 1953–54 that led to the Geneva Conference and the partition of Vietnam.

HALBERSTAM, DAVID. *The Making of a Quagmire*. New York: Random House, 1965. Devastating criticism of the Diem regime by the then *New York Times* correspondent, with a description of the events that led to the overthrow of Diem.

HAMMER, ELLEN J. *The Struggle for Indochina, 1940–1955*. Stanford, Calif.: Stanford University Press, 1966. (The first edition appeared in 1954.) The pioneering work in English on the subject, especially critical of French policy between 1945 and 1953.

HOOPES, TOWNSEND. *The Limits of Intervention*. New York: David McKay Company, 1970. An inside account of how the Johnson policy of escalation in Vietnam was reversed. Particularly important for the information contained in Chapters 8 through 10.

HUARD, PIERRE, and MAURICE DURAND. *Connaissance du Vietnam*. Paris and Hanoi: Imprimerie National, École Française d'Extrême Orient, 1954. A comprehensive study of Vietnamese civilization with introductory chapters on prehistory and history.

ISOART, PAUL. *Le phénomène national vietnamien: De l'indépendance unitaire à l'indépendance fractionnée*. Paris: Librairie Générale de Droit et de Jurisprudence, 1961. A scholarly, up-to-date study of Vietnam in the nineteenth and twentieth centuries.

KAHIN, GEORGE MCTURNAN, and JOHN W. LEWIS. *The United States in Vietnam*. New York: The Dial Press, 1967. The history of U.S. involvement in Vietnam critically analyzed.

KIRK, DONALD. *Wider War: The Struggle for Cambodia, Thailand, and Laos*. London: Pall Mall, and New York: Praeger Publishers, 1971.

LACOUTURE, JEAN. *Ho Chi Minh*. London: Allen Lane The Penguin Press, and New York: Random House, 1968. An up-to-date biography by the well-known French journalist-historian.

————. *Vietnam Between Two Truces*. London: Secher & Warburg, and New York: Random House, 1966. Introduction by JOSEPH KRAFT. Largely articles written over the years on North and South Vietnam, on the founding and composition of the National Liberation Front, and on the decline of the Diem regime.

LANCASTER, DONALD. *The Emancipation of French Indochina*. London and New York: Oxford University Press, 1961. A reliable survey of French Indochina from the period of conquest through the struggle for liberation and the two contemporary Vietnams, by a British diplomat stationed in Saigon during the early 1950's.

LE THANH KHOI. *Le Viet-Nam: Histoire et civilisation*. Paris: Editions de Minuit, 1955. The work of the leading Vietnamese historian of Marxist orientation, covering the entire history from the origin of the Vietnamese nation to 1953.

LURO, ELIACIN. *Le pays d'Annam*. Paris: Leroux, 1897. A fundamental study of the political and social institutions of Vietnam by an early official of the colonial regime.

MCALISTER, JOHN T. JR. *Viet Nam: The Origins of Revolution*. New York: Knopf, 1969. An indispensable analysis for an understanding of contemporary political events in Vietnam.

MARR, DAVID G. *Vietnamese Anti-Colonialism, 1885–1925*. Berkeley, Los Angeles, London: University of California Press, 1971. A pioneering work on the subject in English, based largely on previously untranslated Vietnamese language sources.

MAYBON, CHARLES B. *Histoire moderne du pays d'Annam (1592–1820): Etude sur les premiers rapports des européens et des annamites et sur l'établishsement de la dynastie*. Paris, 1920. Long the standard work in French on Vietnam between the sixteenth and nineteenth centuries.

MECKLIN, JOHN. *Mission in Torment: An Intimate Account of the U.S. Role in Vietnam*. Garden City, N.Y.: Doubleday and Company, 1965. A former high U.S. official in Saigon describes the failure of Diem and the conflict between the U.S. Mission and the American correspondents in Vietnam.

MORGENTHAU, HANS J. *Vietnam and the United States*. Washington, D.C.: Public Affairs Press, 1965. Articles critical of U.S. policy by the noted foreign-policy expert.

MUS, PAUL. *Viet-Nam: Sociologie d'une guerre*. Paris: Éditions du Seuil, 1950. A profound study of the origin and the nature of Vietnamese nationalism and Communism, by the late French expert on Vietnamese history and civilization.

OBERDORFER, DON. *Tet*. Garden City, New York: Doubleday and Company, 1971. The story of a battle and its historical aftermath.

OSBORNE, MILTON. *The French Presence in Cochinchina and Cambodia: Rule and Response 1859–1905*. Ithaca, New York and London: Cornell University Press, 1969. A history of French rule in Southern Vietnam and a comparison of French governmental techniques there with those in Cambodia.

The Pentagon Papers. The complete and unabridged series as published by *The New York Times.* Based on investigative reporting by NEIL SHEEHAN. Written by NEIL SHEEHAN, HEDRICK SMITH, E. W. KENWORTHY, and FOX BUTTERFIELD. With Key Documents and 64 pages of Photographs. New York: Bantam Books, Inc., 1971.

PIKE, DOUGLAS. *Viet Cong.* Cambridge, Mass.: MIT Press, 1966. The main study of the Vietcong, describing the movement as entirely Communist-oriented.

ROBEQUAIN, CHARLES. *The Economic Development of French Indochina.* London: Oxford University Press, 1944. Basic on French economic policy in Indochina. First published in French in 1939.

ROY, JULES. *The Battle of Dien Bien Phu.* New York: Harper and Row, 1965. With an introduction by NEIL SHEEHAN. A veteran French reporter's version of the crucial battle of the Indochina War.

SALISBURY, HARRISON E. *Behind the Lines—Hanoi.* New York: Harper and Row, 1967. The first report by an American visitor to North Vietnam about the effect of the bombing raids.

SCHELL, JONATHAN. *The Military Half: An Account of Destruction in Quang Ngai and Quang Tin.* New York: Knopf, 1968. A description of the effect of bombing raids and artillery fire on the country and people of Vietnam.
——— *The Village of Ben Suc.* New York: Knopf, 1967. Description of the methods used by the U.S. Army in relocating populations.

SCIGLIANO, ROBERT. *South Vietnam: Nation Under Stress.* Boston: Houghton Mifflin Company, 1963. Probably the best report and analysis of the Diem regime.

SHAPLEN, ROBERT. *The Lost Revolution: The U.S. in Vietnam, 1946–1966.* Rev. ed. New York: Harper and Row, 1966. A veteran reporter's account of recent Vietnamese history. Important on the events that led to the fall of Diem.

SULLY, FRANÇOIS, ed. *We the Vietnamese: Voices from Vietnam.* With the Assistance of MARJORIE WEINER NORMAND and a Prefare by DONALD KIRK. New York: Praeger Publishers, 1971. A collection of articles, speeches, and essays on Vietnamese history, customs, culture, art, and literature by Vietnamese authors of both North and South Vietnam.

TABOULET, GEORGES. *La geste française en Indochine.* 2 vols. Paris: Adrien Maisonneuve, 1955 and 1956. Important documents with commentaries by the author on French actions in Indochina prior to the conquest, covering events from the seventeenth to the twentieth century.

THOMPSON, VIRGINIA. *French Indochina.* London: Allen and Unwin, 1937;

New York: Octagon Books, 1967. The standard work on the French colonial regime in Indochina.

The Vietnam Hearings. Introduction by J. WILLIAM FULBRIGHT. New York: Random House, 1966. Important on the Johnson Administration's steps toward military intervention.

WEINSTEIN, FRANKLIN B. *Vietnam's Unheld Elections: The Failure to Carry Out the 1956 Reunification Elections and the Effect on Hanoi's Present Outlook.* Ithaca, N.Y.: Cornell University Press, 1966.

Index

141